THE WORLD OF SILENCE

THE WORLD OF
SILENCE

MAX PICARD

A GATEWAY EDITION
HENRY REGNERY COMPANY
Chicago

The World of Silence was translated by Stanley Godman from *Die Welt des Schweigens*, published in 1948 by Eugen Rentsch Verlag, Erlenbach-Zürich, Switzerland.

FOR ERNST WIECHERT

LINGUA FUNDAMENTUM
SANCTI SILENTII

Inscription on an Altar in Maria-Culm

(*From Goethe's Diaries*)

CONTENTS

ACKNOWLEDGMENTS

Our thanks are due to Messrs. John Lane, The Bodley Head for permission to quote from James Joyce's *Ulysses*; see pages 169-170.

PREFACE

SHALL I confess it? When I first read Max Picard's book, *The World of Silence*, I was disconcerted by it. Everywhere in this book, Picard is talking about silence, talking about it insistently, and with reverence. I could not at first convince myself that the silence he speaks of is something positive, that it is not merely the lack of something. To-day, however, it is no longer so; Picard's book, I think, now touches the same chords, or almost the same chords, in my own soul that it must have touched in his when he conceived it. The fact is that, during the past year, I have become more directly and vividly conscious than ever before of the mystery that is implicit in words as such. I have become aware of what one may call the value for ontology, or for a philosophy of being, of human language; and I owe this awareness perhaps to the few pages in which Heidegger condenses the reflections awakened in him by the reading of Hölderlin and Rilke. I am thinking of such statements as that in Heidegger's "Letter on Humanism": "Language is the dwelling-place of being": that statement would be very difficult to translate into abstract terms, but it undoubtedly expresses an extremely pregnant intuition. And, paradoxical as this may seem, it is only if we start with an

apprehension of the value and reality of language
at the level of a philosophy of being—of the
value of reality not only of language in general
but of the word as such—that we can recognise
what Max Picard means in this book when he
talks about silence.

From the point of view of a hostile critic, of
course—that is to say, from the point of view of
that empirical and evolutionary tradition in philosophy, which has its roots in the last century,
or even more deeply in a prolongation of the
eighteenth century's philosophy of sense-percep-
tion and associationism—Picard's metaphysics of
silence lose any possible meaning; they become
merely absurd. For, to that empiricist philosophy,
the word as such is merely one variety of the
sign. But let us remember that the great Wilhelm
von Humboldt had already affirmed in the most
explicit fashion that language could not be reduced to a mere system of signs, when he said
that, in his opinion, language had to be regarded
as a boon immediately conferred on the human
creature as such. If we accept Humboldt's attitude, it becomes immediately possible to understand—or rather to conceive—how it may be per-
missible to think of the word, as such, coming
forth from the fullness of silence; and how this
fullness of silence confers on the word, as it were,
its legitimate function. Max Picard, for instance,
tells us, that when two human beings converse
together, there is always a third who listens, and

this third is Silence. But such a statement becomes intelligible only if we distinguish between speech, in the true sense, and mere chatter. When two people are merely chattering, there is no longer the third silent listener, or listening silence, perhaps because there is no longer any real person involved in the transaction, but merely a kind of functioning of automatons. Moreover, as Heidegger has also seen very clearly, speech to-day is more and more tending to degenerate into chatter —into what he calls *gerede*. And, given that fact, it is less and less easy for us to recognise the value of silence: its ontological quality, its depth of, or depth in, being.

In Picard's volume, the reader will find a whole set of discussions on such topics as the relation of silence to love, to faith, to poetry—discussions which are each concrete approaches towards that reality which we to-day find it so difficult to reach. We find it difficult just in the degree to which we have lost the sense of the meaning of contemplation—and the very word "contemplation," for most of our contemporaries, has become a dead letter. And on this topic it would be easy to cite the admirable criticism of the discontinuity of existence to-day which Picard himself has put forward in another book of his, *Hitler and Ourselves*.

There is some sense in which silence—in particular the silence of contemplation—unifies present, past, and future; and love, for instance, ex-

presses itself by silence more than by speech; and
that very fact helps us to understand how those
who love each other are, as it were, lifted up
above the level of the merely temporal. The gifts
of premonition and of clairvoyance which are
sometimes granted to those who love each other
are linked, precisely, to this supratemporal quality
of silence.

One could go further; it is, one might say, in
silence that we should seek the native soil in which
faith can grow, or the natural foundations on
which it can be edified. One might say, for instance, that between that unheard of happening,
the Incarnation, and the being of man silence
interposes itself as a kind of buffer; and thus, in
approaching God, man approaches the silence
with which God himself is surrounded. It is a
mark of divine love, writes Max Picard, in a
wonderful sentence, that a mystery of the Faith
always spreads around itself a kind of cloak of
silence. It seems to me that it is above all by taking
such experiences as a starting point—experiences
which partake essentially of the awesome or the
holy—that we can gather to ourselves the deeper
meaning of Max Picard's message. But, on the
other hand, our world is becoming secularised.
And the more it suffers profanation or violation—
words which, for that matter, are ceasing to refer
to anything actual, now that there are no more
sanctuaries—the more this book is in danger of
appearing unintelligible: in danger, even, of re-

ducing itself for the unsympathetic reader to a set of meaningless patterns of mere empty words.

It would be interesting to compare Picard's book with the famous passage about silence that comes, if my memory does not deceive me, into Maeterlinck these days, and one reason for this, I think, is that Maeterlinck was never a real thinker. He was rather a typical man of letters, prowling round and round a thought that he never bothered to make precise; around a thought, indeed, which for him would have lost its attractive halo of mysteriousness if he had ever managed to make it explicit. Picard is just in the opposite case; there are few men to-day who think with more intense concentration than he does, but one should make it clear that his is not a thinking which moves methodically from premises to conclusion but rather, if I may put it so, *a thinking which sees*. One is almost tempted to describe Picard's thought by a technical expression, familiar in the work of Kant and his followers: it is almost an "intellectual intuition." But the phrase "intellectual intuition" smacks too strongly, perhaps, of doctrines of philosophical idealism, which are quite irrelevant in our present context. I am not sure, for all that, that one great early German idealist philosopher, Schelling, in the work of his later years, has not certain profound affinities with Max Picard, as indeed with many other contemporary metaphysicians who have rejected the system-building mania of Hegel.

We should note also that the philosopher to-day, in so far as he is not a merely academic, a merely professorial philosopher, tends to draw nearer to the poet. All around us we can see a new emergence of a lost Atlantis from the depths. On this recovered continent, that unity which thought, as such, and poetry, as such, had in their beginnings is being recreated; and it is on this Atlantis, quite certainly, that Max Picard's work is to be located. Obviously, of course, there are certain fatal confusions that we must avoid here. Max Picard is a Christian, he is a Roman Catholic. Thus the chords which are struck in the soul by such a book as this are entirely different from those struck by Heidegger or even by Rilke: I think that Picard admires the *Elegies from the Castle of Duino* with many reservations.

This, at least, I think one can say without fear of self-deception. All Max Picard's meditative activity is directed towards a kind of possible wholeness of being, and this wholeness is to-day endangered not only by technical progress, but by the will to power of those of whom techniques are only the blind instruments; though they risk seeing these instruments becoming the masters—still, of course, the blind masters—of those whom they are supposed to serve. I doubt myself whether it is possible to exaggerate the seriousness of such warnings, but it should be emphasised that there is nothing in Picard's attitude resembling a nihilistic pessimism. His warnings are rather, in the full sense of the phrase, prophetic affirmations—and he *is* a prophet, in the sense that Péguy and Bloy are. His utterances spring from an eschatological consciousness—from an awareness of the last things, death, judgment, hell, heaven. But what is remarkable is that the tone of his book should nevertheless be so wonderfully peaceful. The silence which he exalts in this book is that of "the peace that passeth all understanding."

GABRIEL MARCEL.

INTRODUCTION

SILENCE IS not simply what happens when we stop talking. It is more than the mere negative renunciation of language; it is more than simply a condition that we can produce at will.

When language ceases, silence begins. But it does not begin *because* language ceases. The absence of language simply makes the presence of Silence more apparent.

Silence is an autonomous phenomenon. It is therefore not identical with the suspension of language. It is not merely the negative condition that sets in when the positive is removed; it is rather an independent whole, subsisting in and through itself. It is creative, as language is creative; and it is formative of human beings as language is formative, but not in the same degree.

Silence belongs to the basic structure of man.

It is not the intention of this book, however, that the reader should be led to a "Philosophy of Silence," nor that he should be misled into despising language. It is language and not silence that makes man truly human. The word has supremacy over silence.

But language becomes emaciated if it loses its connection with silence. Our task, therefore, is to

uncover the world of silence so obscured today—
not for the sake of silence but for the sake of
language.

It may seem surprising that anything can be said
about silence through the medium of language,
but only if one thinks of silence as something
completely negative. Silence is, on the contrary, a
positive, a reality, and language has the power to
make assertions about all reality.

Language and silence belong together: language
has knowledge of silence as silence has knowledge
of language.

THE WORLD OF SILENCE

THE NATURE OF SILENCE

SILENCE IS nothing merely negative; it is not the mere absence of speech. It is a positive, a complete world in itself.

Silence has greatness simply because it is. It *is*, and that is its greatness, its pure existence.

There is no beginning to silence and no end: it seems to have its origins in the time when everything was still pure Being. It is like uncreated, everlasting Being.

When silence is present, it is as though nothing but silence had ever existed.

Where silence is, man is observed by silence. Silence looks at man more than man looks at silence. Man does not put silence to the test; silence puts man to the test.

One cannot imagine a world in which there is nothing but language and speech, but one can imagine a world where there is nothing but silence.

Silence contains everything within itself. It is not waiting for anything; it is always wholly present in itself and it completely fills out the space in which it appears.

It does not develop or increase in time, but time increases in silence. It is as though time had been sown into silence, as though silence had absorbed it; as though silence were the soil in which time grows to fullness.

Silence is not visible, and yet its existence is clearly apparent. It extends to the farthest distances, yet is so close to us that we can feel it as concretely as we feel our own bodies. It is intangible, yet we can feel it as directly as we feel materials and fabrics. It cannot be defined in words, yet it is quite definite and unmistakable.

In no other phenomenon are distance and nearness, range and immediacy, the all-embracing and the particular, so united as they are in silence.

2

Silence is the only phenomenon today that is "useless." It does not fit into the world of profit and utility; it simply *is*. It seems to have no other purpose; it cannot be exploited.

All the other great phenomena have been appropriated by the world of profit and utility. Even the space between heaven and earth has become a mere cavity for aeroplanes to travel through. Water and fire have been absorbed by the world of profit; they are only noticed in so far as they are parts of this world: they have lost their independent existence.

Silence, however, stands outside the world of

profit and utility; it cannot be exploited for profit; you cannot get anything out of it. It is "unproductive." Therefore it is regarded as valueless.

Yet there is more help and healing in silence than in all the "useful things." Purposeless, un-exploitable silence suddenly appears at the side of the all-too-purposeful, and frightens us by its very purposelessness. It interferes with the regular flow of the purposeful. It strengthens the untouchable, it lessens the damage inflicted by exploitation. It makes things whole again, by taking them back from the world of dissipation into the world of wholeness. It gives things something of its own holy uselessness, for that is what silence is: holy uselessness.

3

Above all things, it is necessary that one should leave untouched the virgin soil, divinely built according to pure law. (Hölderlin)

Here in silence is the Holy Wilderness, because the wilderness and the building of God are one. There is no movement here to be regulated by the law: existence and activity are one in silence. It is as though the whole orbit of a star were to be suddenly concentrated into a single light: that is the unity of existence and activity concentrated in silence.

Silence gives to things inside it something of

the power of its own autonomous being. The autonomous being in things is strengthened in silence. That which is developable and exploitable in things vanishes when they are in silence.

Through this power of autonomous being, silence points to a state where only being is valid: the state of the Divine. The mark of the Divine in things is preserved by their connection with the world of silence.

THE BASIC PHENOMENON
OF SILENCE

SILENCE IS a basic phenomenon. That is to say, it is a primary, objective reality, which cannot be traced back to anything else. It cannot be replaced by anything else; it cannot be exchanged with anything else. There is nothing behind it to which it can be related except the Creator Himself.

Silence is original and self-evident like the other basic phenomena; like love and loyalty and death and life itself. But it existed before all these and is in all of them. Silence is the firstborn of the basic phenomena. It envelops the other basic phenomena—love, loyalty, and death; and there is more silence than speech in them, more of the invisible than the visible. There is also more silence in one person than can be used in a single human life. That is why every human utterance is surrounded by a mystery. The silence in a man stretches out beyond the single human life. In this silence man is connected with past and future generations.

The basic phenomena take us, as it were, back to the beginning of things; we have left behind

us, what Goethe called "the merely derived phenomena" with which we normally live. It is like
a death, for we are left on our own, faced with
a new beginning—and so we are afraid. "When
the basic phenomena are revealed to our senses
we feel a kind of shyness and even fear itself,"
Goethe said. In silence, therefore, man stands
confronted once again by the original beginning
of all things: everything can begin again, everything can be re-created. In every moment of
time, man through silence can be with the origins of all things. Allied with silence, man par-
ticipated not only in the original substance of
silence but in the original substance of all things.
Silence is the only basic phenomenon that is always at man's disposal. No other basic phenomenon is so present in every moment as silence.

Sexuality is the other basic phenomenon that
is always at man's disposal. Since the basic phenomenon of silence has been destroyed today,
man depends too much on the basic phenomenon of sexuality, and he fails to notice that sexuality loses all proportion and becomes false
when it is not safe and out of danger in its
proper place among the other basic phenomena,
and is not kept in order.

Still like some old, forgotten animal from the
beginning of time, silence towers above all the
puny world of noise; but as a living animal, not
an extinct species, it lies in wait, and we can still

see its broad back sinking ever deeper among the briers and bushes of the world of noise. It is as though this prehistoric creature were gradually sinking into the depths of its own silence. And yet sometimes all the noise of the world today seems like the mere buzzing of insects on the broad back of silence.

SILENCE AS THE ORIGIN
OF SPEECH

I

Speech came out of silence, out of the fullness of silence. The fullness of silence would have exploded if it had not been able to flow out into speech.

The speech that comes out of silence is as it were justified by the silence that precedes it. It is the spirit that legitimizes speech, but the silence that precedes speech is the pregnant mother who is delivered of speech by the creative activity of the spirit. The sign of this creative activity of the spirit is the silence that precedes speech.

Whenever a man begins to speak, the word comes from silence at each new beginning.

It comes so self-evidently and so unobtrusively as if it were merely the reverse of silence, merely silence turned around. Speech is in fact the reverse of silence, just as silence is the reverse of speech.

There is something silent in every word, as an abiding token of the origin of speech. And in every silence there is something of the spoken word, as an abiding token of the power of silence to create speech.

Speech is therefore essentially related to silence.

Not until one man speaks to another, does he learn that speech no longer belongs to silence but to man. He learns it through the *Thou* of the other person, for through the *Thou* the word first belongs to man and no longer to silence. When two people are conversing with one another, however, a third is always present: Silence is listening. That is what gives breadth to a conversation: when the words are not moving merely within the narrow space occupied by the two speakers, but come from afar, from the place where silence is listening. That gives the words a new fullness. But not only that: the words are spoken as it were *from* the silence, from that third person, and the listener receives more than the speaker alone is able to give. Silence is the third speaker in such a conversation. At the end of the Platonic dialogues it is always as though silence itself were speaking. The persons who were speaking seem to have become listeners to silence.

2

At the beginning of creation, we are told, God Himself spoke with man. It was as though man still did not really dare to speak the word, did not yet dare to possess the word; as though God, by speaking with man, wanted to get man into the habit of using words.

When we recall the beauty, the might and the manifoldness of language, ranging over the whole earth, there seems something almost superhuman in it, something that does not seem to have had its origin in man, something the perfection of which man has in fact corrupted and destroyed. (Jakob Grimm)

The origin of language is impenetrable, like that of every creature, because it came from the perfect love of the Creator. Only if man were to live constantly in perfect love, could he learn the origin of language and of all creatures.

3

The clearly defined and wholly immediate word arises from the indefinite, far-ranging pre-historic realm of silence.

Silence reveals itself in a thousand inexpressible forms: in the quiet of dawn, in the noiseless aspiration of trees towards the sky, in the stealthy descent of night, in the silent changing of the seasons, in the falling moonlight, trickling down into the night like a rain of silence, but above all in the silence of the inward soul,—all these forms of silence are nameless: all the clearer and surer is the word that arises out of and in contrast to the nameless silence.

There is no greater natural world than the natural world of silence; no greater world of spirit than the linguistic world of spirit formed by the natural world of silence.

Silence is a world in itself, and from this world of silence speech learns to form itself into a world: the world of silence and the world of speech confront each other. Speech is therefore opposed to silence, but not as an enemy: it is only the other side, the reverse of silence. One can hear silence sounding through speech. Real speech is in fact nothing but the resonance of silence.

4

The sound of music is not, like the sound of words, opposed, but rather parallel to silence.

It is as though the sounds of music were being driven over the surface of silence.

Music is silence, which in dreaming begins to sound.

Silence is never more audible than when the last sound of music has died away.

Music is far-ranging, and could occupy the

whole of space. This does not in fact happen, for music occupies space very slowly, shyly, rhythmically, always returning to the same basic melodies so that it might seem that the sounds of music never moved away at all, that music were everywhere and yet always in a definite limited place. In music the distance and the nearness of space, the limitless and the limited are all together in one gentle unity that is a comfort and a benefaction to the soul. For however far the soul may range in music it is everywhere protected and brought home safely again. That is also why music has such a calming effect on nervous people: it brings a wideness to the soul in which the soul can be without fear.

5

Language is a world, not a mere appendage to another world. It has a fullness that goes out beyond the limits of the expedient: there is more in language than would be necessary for mere understanding and information.

It is true that language belongs to man, but it also belongs to itself. There is more pain and joy and sadness in it than man can get out of it for himself. It is as though, independently of man, language keeps back enough pain, sadness, joy, and jubilation for itself.

Language sometimes creates poetry of its own accord and as it were all for itself.

6

Silence can exist without speech, but speech cannot exist without silence. The word would be without depth if the background of silence were missing. Nevertheless silence is not more than speech; on the contrary, silence on its own, the world of silence without speech, is the world *before* creation, the world of unfinished creation, a world of menace and danger to man. Not until speech comes out of silence does silence come out of pre-creation into creation, out of the pre-historic into the history of man, into close relationship with man, becoming part of man and a lawful part of speech. But speech is more than silence, because truth is first expressed concretely by speech, not by silence.

It is through speech that man first becomes man:

> Is it a coincidence that the Greeks defined the nature of man as ξῷον λόγον ἔχων? The later interpretation of this definition of man in the sense of "animal rationale," the living being endowed with reason, is not wrong, but it hides the phenomenal soil from which this definition of existence is taken. "Man reveals himself as the being that speaks." (Heidegger)

Silence is fulfilled only when speech comes forth from silence. Speech gives it meaning and honour. Through speech, silence, that wild, pre-human monster, is transformed into something tame and human.

The outward face of speech is thus: it is like solid blocks of lava erupted from the surface of silence, lying scattered about and connected one with another by the surface of silence.

And as the mass of the sea is greater than the mass of the land, so that of silence is greater than that of speech. But just as the mainland has more being than the sea, so speech is more powerful than silence; it has a greater intensity of being.

7

Silence is woven into the very texture of human nature, but it is only the basis on which the higher appears.

In the human mind silence is merely knowledge of the *Deus absconditus*, the hidden god.

In the human spirit silence is merely the silent harmony with things and the audible harmony of music.

In the human body silence is the fount of beauty.

But as beauty is more than the physical body, and music more than the inaudible ground of the spirit, and the revealed God more than the Deus Absconditus, so speech is more than silence.

8

Of his own accord, man would never have been able to create speech out of silence. Speech is so completely different from silence that man himself would never have been able to make the leap from silence to speech.

The fact that two contrary phenomena like silence and speech are so closely allied as to seem to belong together, could never have been achieved by man, but only by an act of God Himself. The contiguity of silence and speech is a sign of that Divine state in which they are perfectly united.

It was inevitable that speech should come out of silence. For since Christ the Divine Word came down to men from God, the "still small voice," the way of the transformation of silence into speech was traced out for all time. The Word that appeared two thousand years ago was on the way to man from the beginning of time, and therefore from the very beginning there was a breach between silence and speech. The event of two thousand years ago was so miraculous that all silence from time immemorial was torn open by speech. Silence trembled in advance of the event and broke in two.

SILENCE, LANGUAGE AND
TRUTH

I

LANGUAGE is more than silence because truth is manifested in language. There is truth in silence, too, but it is not so characteristic of silence as it is of language that truth is present in it. Truth is in silence only in so far as silence participates in the truth that is in the order of being in general. In silence truth is passive and slumbering, but in language it is wide-awake; and in language active decisions are made concerning truth and falsehood.

In itself, by its nature, language is only of short duration, like a break in the continuity of silence. It is truth that gives it continuity, that enables it to become a world of its own; it is because it receives this continuity from truth that language does not pass away. The silence out of which language came is now transformed into the mystery surrounding truth.

Without truth language would be a general fog of words above the silence; without truth it would collapse into an indistinct murmuring. It is truth that makes language clear and firm. The line separating the true from the false is the support that holds language back from falling. Truth is the scaffolding that gives language an independent foothold over against silence. Language becomes a world of its own, as we have said already; and language now has not only a world behind it—the world of silence, but a world near at hand—the world of truth.

The word of truth must keep in *rapport* with silence, however, for without it truth would be too harsh and too hard. It would then seem as though there were only one *single* truth, since the austerity of the individual truth would suggest a denial of the inter-relatedness of all truth. The essential point about truth is that it all hangs together in an all-embracing context.

The nearness of silence means also the nearness of forgiveness and the nearness of love, for the natural basis of forgiveness and of love is silence. It is important that this natural basis should be there, for it means that forgiveness and love do not have first to create the medium in which they appear.

2

"There is no truth," said one. The other said: "But you are yourself assuming that it is a truth that there is no truth."

The logical force displayed in this sentence is an indication that through the logic that is in language from the very beginning, truth is automatically manifest in language. Through its very structure language brings truth to man: truth presses itself on him before he seeks it out for himself.

This is another sign that man did not acquire language on his own account, but that it was given to him by a Being that is Truth itself.

Language corresponds by its very structure to the truth that is made manifest in it. Therefore every thing has an impulse to be expressed in language, because it finds fulfilment in language and is raised to a higher level through the truth. There is an incline from silence to language, to the truth of the word; and the gravitational force of this incline pushes truth on still further from language down into the active life of the world.

Truth is present as an objective reality in the logic of language, and this given objective reality refers man to something outside himself, to the objective in general. When he speaks, man is reminded of the certainty of an objectively given truth.

Through this objectivity that is in language, there is more in language than the individual (i.e., the subject) can take out, more than the individual needs. There is so much objective reality in language that it will last to the end of human history and beyond.

Because of this objectivity in language, more

is often expressed than the speaker intends, and therefore man often learns more from language than he puts into it with his own thoughts.

Man is therefore exalted by language because it is more than man himself.

It is part of the nature of man that he is not able to express the whole of truth in words. To fill the empty spaces in language which are not filled with truth, he brings in sorrow. Sorrow can stretch out a word to the silence in which it sinks to rest and oblivion.

Only Christ was able to fill speech brimful with truth. This is why His words are not melancholy: in Him the space of language is filled with nothing but truth. There is no room left for sorrow or for melancholy.

3

There is a radiance surrounding truth, and this radiance is a sign that truth has an impulse to expand in all directions.

The radiance surrounding truth is beauty. In this way truth is able to penetrate far and wide; the radiance of beauty prepares the way for truth; it occupies all space in advance of truth and for truth. The truth is already present everywhere, *in partibus infidelium*.

Beauty is also present in silence; it is primarily in silence. Silence would sink weighted down into its own darkness, down to the abyss, dragging down with it much that belongs to the brightness of earth, if beauty were not also present in silence. Beauty gives a lightness and airiness to silence, so that it, too, becomes a part of the brightness of earth. Beauty relieves silence of its heaviness, brings it up into the light of earth and brings it to man. The radiance of the beauty which rests on silence is a premonition of the radiance inhering in the word of truth.

In the God-Man the Word, the Truth, and the radiance of Perfect Beauty are a unity. One is not behind the other or even beside the other, but all are one in a perfect unity. And in this unity all history meets in one Person: the beginning of man, his sin, and his redemption.

THE SILENCE IN SPEECH

SPEECH AND silence belong together. To see speech without silence is like seeing Shakespeare's fools without the solidity of Shakespeare's heroes, or like seeing the martyrdom of the saints in medieval pictures without their transfiguration. Speech and silence, hero and fool, martyrdom and transfiguration—all are a unity.

Speech must remain in relationship with the silence from which it raised itself up. It belongs to human nature that speech should turn back to silence, for it belongs to human nature to return to the place whence it has come.

Human speech is determined not only by truth but also by goodness: in goodness speech returns to its origin.

It is important that speech remain in relationship with silence through goodness, for it means that from the very beginning goodness is part of the texture of every word, that in the very structure of language there is an inclination towards goodness. In the word that was related to the greatest silence was the greatest goodness.

Words that merely come from other words are

hard and aggressive. Such words are also lonely, and a great part of the melancholy in the world today is due to the fact that man has made words lonely by separating them from silence. This repudiation of silence is a factor of human guilt, and the melancholy in the world is the outward expression of that guilt. Language is surrounded by the dark rim of melancholy, no longer by the rim of silence.

Silence is present in language, therefore, even after language has arisen out of silence. The world of language is built over and above the world of silence. Language can only enjoy security as it moves about freely in words and ideas in so far as the broad world of silence is stretched out below. From the breadth of silence language learns to achieve its own breadth. Silence is for language what the net stretched out taut below him is for the tightrope walker.

The mind, the infinite mind that is in language, needs to have below it the infinity of silence so that it can build its own arch of infinity over it. It is quite possible for the mind to be infinite and immeasurable of its own accord. But the silence underneath helps it to move freely in its own infinity.

Silence is the natural basis for the immeasurable infinity of mind. It is the natural basis for the mind in any case: that which is unutterable in the language of the mind connects the mind with silence, makes it at home in the world of silence.

Language must remain in intimate relationship with silence. The transparent, hovering way of silence makes language itself transparent and hovering. It is like a bright cloud over silence, a bright cloud over the placid lake of silence.

Silence provides a natural source of re-creation for language, a source of refreshment and purification from the wickedness to which language itself has given rise. In silence language holds its breath and fills its lungs with pure and original air.

Even when language remains the same, it is able to appear as something original and new as it emerges from silence. Truth, which is always expressed in the same words, does not therefore become solidified.

The spirit it also able to give to language refreshing draughts of new life. There is a kind of refreshment that comes from contact with natural silence, and another kind that is produced by the spirit. Perfection is achieved when the original power and freshness of the natural silence and of the spirit meet and are combined in one person, as in Dante and Goethe.

Now thou has finished thine appointed task here below, stern Mind, and a gentle playful sun has streamed into the last evening storm on thy breast and filled the storm with roses and gold. The

globe and all earthly things from which the fleeting worlds are formed were much too small and
light for thee. For thou wast searching for something higher than life behind life, not thine own
self, no mortal or immortal being but the Eternal,
the Alpha, the God—the appearance of the things
of this world below, both the evil and the good,
was so indifferent to thee. Now thou art resting in
the real world of being, death has taken from thy
dark heart the whole sultry cloud of life and the
eternal Light stands uncovered, the Light thou
hast sought so long; and thou, one of its rays,
dwellest once again in the fire. (Jean Paul, *Titan*)

These words of Jean Paul are like round bal-
loons controlled invisibly from below by silence.
It is as though everything said here aloud in
words had already happened in silence, for that
is what gives the words their quality of sure certainty, intimacy and sublimity. As if in a dream
the words imitate the movements that have already happened in the silence.

In Goethe language assumes a more self-conscious attitude towards silence than in Jean
Paul. It is the victory of language over silence
which is supremely important, not in the sense
of a boastful triumph but in the sense of the consciousness and pride of a man who knows that it
is language that has first made him a man and
who therefore shows pride in his use of words.

2

Man lives between the world of silence from which he comes and the world of the other silence to which he goes—the world of death. Human language also lives between these two worlds of silence and is upheld by them. That is why language has a double echo: from the place whence it came and from the place of death.

Language receives innocence, simplicity, and originality from the silence whence it came, but its short duration, its fragility, and the fact that language never entirely corresponds to the things it is describing, come from the second silence, from death.

The marks of both worlds are evident in the language of Jean Paul: the innocence and originality, and at the same time the readiness to depart, and the fleeting transience of language.

In the modern world language is far from both worlds of silence. It springs from noise and vanishes in noise. Silence is today no longer an autonomous world of its own; it is simply the place into which noise has not yet penetrated. It is a mere interruption of the continuity of noise, like a technical hitch in the noise-machine—that is what silence is today: the momentary breakdown of noise. We no longer have definite si-

lence and definite language, but simply words
that are being spoken and words that have not
yet been spoken—but these are present, too,
standing around like tools that are not being
used; they stand waiting there menacingly or
boringly.

The other silence, the silence of death, is also
absent in language today, just as real death is
absent in the modern world. Death is no longer
an autonomous world of its own, but merely
something negative: the extreme end of what
we call life: life emptied to the last dregs—that
is what death is today. Death itself has been
killed. Death today is far removed from that
death of which the following sentence was
spoken:

> Man dies only once in his life, and as he lacks
> experience of the event he bungles it. So that he
> may die successfully, he must learn how to die by
> following the instruction of experienced men who
> know what it means to die in the midst of life.
> Asceticism gives us this experience of death.
> (Florensky)

When language is no longer related to silence
it loses its source of refreshment and renewal
and therefore something of its substance. Language today seems to talk automatically, out of
its own strength, and, emptying and scattering
itself, it seems to be hastening to an end. There
is something hard and obstinate in language today, as though it were making a great effort to

remain alive in spite of its emptiness. There is also something desperate in it, as though it were expecting its emptiness to lead it to a relentless end, and it is this alternation of obstinacy and despair which makes it so restless. By taking it away from silence we have made language an orphan. The tongue we speak today is no longer a mother-tongue but rather an orphaned tongue. It sometimes seems as though man were ashamed of the language he has separated from its parent: man hardly feels he can dare to communicate his words to another. He talks more to himself and into himself, as though he wanted to crush, crumple, and destroy the words he speaks and throw them like ruins down into the emptiness of his own soul.

It is only in the language of the poets that the real word, the word connected with silence, still sometimes appears. It is like a ghost, full of sadness that it is only a ghost and must disappear again. Beauty is the dark cloud in which such words appear only to disappear again.

3

Language sinks down again into the silence. It can be forgotten. There is an oblivion in language, it seems, so that language should not be too violent. The supremacy that language has over silence is thereby mitigated.

The sinking of words into oblivion is as it were a sign that things belong to us only temporarily and can be called back to whence they came.

When a word sinks into oblivion, it is forgotten, and this forgetting prepares the way for forgiveness. That is a sign that love is woven into the very structure of language: words sink into the forgetfulness of man so that in forgetting he may also forgive.

The disappearance and forgetting of a word also prepares the way for death. Just as the word that makes us human disappears, so man himself dies: death also is woven into the very structure of language.

Today it seems as though language had been robbed of its forgetfulness: every word is present somewhere in the general noise of words around us. In the general noise of words everything emerges for a moment, only to disappear again. Everything is there at the same time and yet not there at all. There is no longer any present immediacy of the word and therefore no forgetting. Forgetting is no longer done by man directly but proceeds outside his control in the general noise of words jostling one with another. But that is not a forgetting at all, but merely a disappearing. And so there is no forgiving either in the world today; since now one can never get *rid* of a word or a thing, it is always bound to turn up again somewhere. And it is also a fact that one never really *has* a word or a thing to-day—and that is why people are so nervous.

4

We have said that language comes from silence and returns to silence. It is as though behind silence were the absolute word to which, through silence, human language moves. It is as though the human word were sustained by the absolute word. Because it is there, the human word is not scattered as the dust. Man would have to be constantly regaining the realm of language if it were not secured from attack in the absolute word. All human words seem to move around that word.

Silence is like a remembrance of that word. The different languages are like different attempts to find the absolute word. It is as though words had agreed to divide themselves up into various languages, in order to attempt the discovery of the absolute word from different directions. Languages seem to be like so many expeditions to find the absolute word.

If there were only one language, this language would be in a much too triumphant position in regard to silence. Language would seem too much like territory conquered from silence, and silence too much subject to the will of language.

Man might become arrogant about this one extraordinary conquest. In fact he did become arrogant when all men had only one language:

> Behold, the people is one, and they have all one language; and this they begin to do: and now nothing will be restrained from them, which they have imagined to do. (Gen. 11:6)

As soon as there are many languages, however, languages are inter-related. No single is exclusive; each is merely one among many.

The extraordinary thing is now no longer the existence of a single language but that truth is mediated through many languages. There is now a new unity of languages based on the fact that the one truth is expressed through all languages.

MAN BETWEEN SILENCE
AND SPEECH

I

IN THE MOMENT before man speaks, language still hovers over the silence it has just left; it hovers between silence and speech. The word is still uncertain where to turn: whether to return wholly into the silence and vanish therein or whether to make a clear break with silence by becoming a sound. Human freedom decides whither the word shall go.

As opposed to the word that is in silence, the spoken word is not merely communication with another person. It is qualitatively different from the word that is in silence. By becoming sound a word is not merely drawn out of the silence and communicated to others, but rather set off against the other words that are still in the silence. The spoken word isolates an idea more than it is isolated in the silence, for in the moment in which it is spoken aloud it stands apart and receives a special value of its own. An idea that is in the silence may very well be clearly marked off from all other ideas, but the decision as to which idea or ideas shall receive special prominence and value has not yet been made. While the words are still enclosed in silence, man has not yet taken the risk of a firm decision. Not until the word is spoken or written does man identify himself absolutely with the word.

The word that is in the silence dwells in a world that transcends the world of sight—that is the world of silence. The gleam of transparency that the word has comes from the gleam of that invisible world, the gleam that descends on the word when it is still enclosed in human silence.

2

Silence calls forth sadness in man, for it reminds him of that state in which the fall caused by the word had not yet taken place. Silence makes man yearn for that state before the fall of man, and at the same time it makes him anxious, for in the silence it is as though any moment the word may suddenly appear and with the word the first fall into sin take place again. That is why men regard the poet as presumptuous because he, the poet, whose only material is language, does not seem to bother about the fact that man fell from the word into sin. But man also feels himself drawn to the poet because the word is still in its original state in poetry, like the very first word that made him man; and this makes him happy.

3

When man is silent he finds himself, not subjectively but phenomenologically, in the state that preceded the creation of language. That is to say, when a man is silent he is like man awaiting the creation of language for the first time. It is true that in the silence man has the word, but the word is almost on the point of vanishing. In the silence man is as it were ready to give the word back to the Creator from whom he first received it. Therefore there is something holy in almost every silence.

In silence man is as one who is on the point of returning the word to whence it came. But in the next moment, the moment in which he speaks, he is as one who has just received the word from the silence. In the silence man almost ceases to be man but he comes back again with the speaking of the first word. If one considers closely a man who begins to speak after a long silence, it is as though before one's own eyes he had just been created man through the word, re-confirmed as man by the word.

Out of the silence, again and again, as though by a creative act, comes the word, the absolutely other. This creative act thereby becomes embodied in the basic structure of man.

Creativeness is so much part of man that we cannot regard it as something exceptional and peculiar in man, but rather as the normal characteristic that makes man man in the first place, like speech. Creativeness is just as much part of the basic human structure as speech.

If, however, speech loses its connection with silence, then in the place formerly occupied by silence there is only the emptiness of the abyss. Language disappears into this emptiness as formerly into silence. Words are absorbed by the emptiness, and a monstrous fear arises in man that he may cease to be man when the last word has vanished into the emptiness of the abyss.

4

Here, therefore, in the silence man lives between his destruction (since silence can be the beginning of the absolute loss of the word) and his resurrection.

This is the central place of Faith: in the silence it is as though man were ready to surrender the word through which he became man, and return it to God from whom he received it, believing that he will receive it back again.

Here in this central place Pascal destroyed himself before he rose again as the Pascal of the *Mémorial* and the *Pensées*. After the destruction, he was like a man receiving the word for the first time.

He could speak only in fragments; every sentence in the *Mémorial* and the *Pensées* is like the first sentence ever.

It is as though he wanted always to begin where he himself was begun, as though he wanted to repeat again and again and never to leave that unique event through which he received the word as for the first time and through which he rose again from the death of the spirit. These fragments are no mere fragments but the sum total of the resurrection of man.

THE DEMONIC IN SILENCE
AND SPEECH

I

In SILENCE there is present not only the power of healing and friendship but also the power of darkness and terror, that which can erupt from the underground of silence, the power of death and evil. "Le silence éternel de ces espaces infinis m'effraie" (Pascal).

The word that comes from silence is in danger of contact with the destructive and demonic power that is in silence. Every moment something subterranean and menacing can appear in the word and push out the friendliness and peace that also want to emerge from the silence into the word.

But this menacing power of the demonic can only invade the word, can only find space in the word when the word is not filled with the spirit. For the power of the spirit in the word can overcome the demonic. The fear is taken out of silence, it is banished, by the word in which the spirit dwells—that is, in which truth and order dwell. The demonic element in silence is tamed by the spirit of truth and order, and silence then follows the word like a useful, obedient animal: it helps the word by giving it something of the original power and nourishment that is in silence.

We speak therefore in a language that has been liberated from the power of the demonic by the spirit. Man is partly saved from the incursion of the demonic by language in which the spirit is at work.

In the spirit that is in the word there is preserved a mark of the divine Logos; it is that which gives the word the power to bring the demonic into subjection.

But if the word has lost connection with the spirit it is exposed to all the powers of the demonic, including the demonic that can come to it from the underground of silence. Silence is then no longer silent for the sake of the word but for its own sake only: it stands menacingly against the word, and the fear comes over man that silence may take away from him the word and even the sound of the word.

Man sometimes uses the elemental demonic power in silence: when the examining magistrate sits for hours on end in silence opposite the criminal, the natural demonic power of silence becomes so great that the accused's will is no longer capable of hiding its secrets. The disguise is broken and the truth revealed.

2

The origin of language is "a prehistoric act, of which we can know nothing" (*Scheler*), but it is a prehistoric act like the subjection of the Titans and the pre-Olympic gods: if it had not been for the victory of the Olympic gods the powers of subterranean darkness would have prevailed on the earth. But for the victory of the spirit that is in the word over the demonic power that is in silence, silence would have taken possession of everything and laid it waste.

Before the creation of the word, silence had occupied everything. The earth belonged to silence. It was as though the earth were built on and over silence; it was merely the edge of silence. Then came the word. Demonic silence sank into ruin, but it seemed as if after all the earth would have to be torn from silence piece by piece as clearings are made in the primeval forest. From the primeval forest of silence arose, through the spirit that is in the word, the *friendly* ground of silence which feeds and carries the word.

But in the night the elemental force in silence sometimes becomes all-powerful. It is then as though an invasion of the word were being prepared. The dark forest appears as the place where silence is gathering its forces for the attack. The bright walls of the house seem like the tombstones of the word. Then a light appears upstairs in the room of a house, and it is as though the word were being spoken for the very first time. The whole colossus of silence lies waiting for its master like an obedient animal.

3

In the following poem by Matthias Claudius the power of language over the demonism of the silence of the night is revealed:

> Der Mond ist aufgegangen,
> die goldenen Sternlein prangen
> am Himmel hell und klar;
> der Wald steht schwarz und schweiget,
> und aus den Wiesen steiget
> der weisse Nebel wunderbar.

In this poem the demonic silence of night is overcome by the brightness of language. Moon and stars, forest, meadows and mist all find and meet each other in the clear light of the word. The night becomes so clear in the light of the poem that moon and stars, forest meadows and mist find their way to the daylight from which the word descended. The silence is now no longer dark: it has been made transparent by the light and radiance of the word that falls on the silence. Through the word the silence ceases to be in demonic isolation and becomes the friendly sister of the word.

LANGUAGE AND GESTURE

It is wrong to derive language from gesture
(Condillac, Maine de Biran, Bergson). Gesture
belongs to a totally different category from language. It is not distinct from the passions by
which it is caused: it is mixed up with them. It is
part of them and usually expresses a desire.
Language, on the other hand, expresses a *being*,
a whole, not merely a desire that is only a part of
being and not a whole being in itself. There is in
it more of the substance of whole being than
passion and desire. Language is in fact such an
uncommon being that it creates being itself. Gesture, on the other hand, has no independent
store of being from which it can draw to give to
other phenomena. It scurries along with no independent existence of its own.

Man would never have been able to reach
language over the stepping stones of gesture, for
gesture has something of the unredeemed about
it, and only through a special creative act can it
give rise to something free. Language is clear
and free and sovereign, rising above itself and
leaving everything behind it except the silence
from which it comes. Gesture, on the other hand,
is unfree, unredeemed, still completely mixed

with the material it uses in its attempts at self-representation. It is still inside the material and bound up with it, not approaching the material freely from outside as the spirit approaches the word.

> Gesture has the hollowness and gloom of the physiological and psychological reflexes from which it is born and which it releases in its turn (which is the basis of its intelligibility); it has not the clarity and brightness of language. (Bauhofer)

It is true that gesture precedes language in the child, but that is not the essential point at all. The essential point is the appearance of language in the child quite independently of the gesture that precedes it, and oblivious of the previous existence of gesture. The precedence of gesture is not the point, but rather the fact that by a creative act each new child is redeemed from gesture.

Language belongs absolutely to the eternal world of being—so much so that the genetic factor in language is unimportant, being as it were swallowed up by the power of being. Even if language had developed slowly, "becoming" would not have to be taken into account, being completely absorbed by the world of being.

> The observant eye of any spiritual being noticing the gradual development and perfection of the animal world as we see it from form to form would, before it reached man, draw this con-

clusion: the voice that sounded so splendidly in the bird moves toward gradual extinction in the mammal, and a creature beyond the ape would necessarily be completely voiceless. This is, however, often and almost always the way of the higher creative power: that it scatters the blessings and wonders of a higher level of life and allows them to develop in those places where the old life seemed dead, and that it calls forth its new creations from the dead. (G. H. von Schubert)

Language belongs to human life itself, is part of it, merged and blended with it.

Language must, in accordance with my deepest conviction, be considered part of the very constitution of man. In order truly to understand one single word, not as a merely physical stimulant but as an articulated sound describing a concept, language must reside in man as a whole and as a coherent structure. (W. von Humboldt)

Language can be derived only from another being and from a Being that is still more powerful than the being of language.

THE ANCIENT LANGUAGES

I

IN THE FABLES of the Golden Age we are told that men understood the language of all animals, trees, flowers, and grasses. That is a reminder of the fact that in the *first* language that had just come from the fullness of silence, there was still the all-containing fullness.

This language climbed upwards toward the vault of heaven at the same time.

It formed an arch over all the sounds of the earth, and all the sounds of the whole of nature met together. As everything that rises from the earth is taken up into the vault of heaven, so all the voices of the earth were taken up by the one heaven of language. Every single voice entered in and became a part of it, and therefore every voice was understood. This heaven of the languages was the homeland of all voices; they all came to themselves and to each other in this heaven. This language was unobtrusive despite its powerfulness, as unobtrusive as silence itself.

2

The ancient languages are constructed radially, always beginning from and returning to the centre that is silence, like a fountain with its jets all starting in an arc from the centre, returning to it and disappearing in it.

In modern writings the idea seems to arise from the movements of a man walking straight forward. In the writings of the ancients on the other hand it seems to arise from that of a bird hovering and advancing in circles. (Joubert)

In the early languages there was a mixture of reticence and power: reticence and shyness because language had only just emerged from silence, and power because it had to make sure of its position, to establish itself so that it could not be swept back into silence.

A quiver full of steel arrows, a firmly secured anchor rope, a brazen trumpet splitting the air with its few piercing tones: that is the Hebrew language—it can say but little, but what it says is like the beating of hammers on the anvil. (Renan, *Israel*)

Almost unchangeable, like a piece of the Cyclopean wall, the ancient words stand as if waiting, as if they might be called back into silence just as they were sent out of silence. It is as though they felt themselves still under the con-

trol of silence, as if they were still glancing backwards to the silence whence they came. It was
also always possible that another, higher word, a
corrective, might come out of the silence.

The early languages had to secure a firm position for themselves—and they were therefore
static. The individual words were like stakes set
in the ground, each one on its own, with hardly
any connection between one stake and the next.
The architecture of the language was vertical.
Each word sank down vertically, column-wise,
into the sentence.

> In our old laws the language usually sounds grave
> and strong; less abrupt, less curt, rather slow and
> yet without dragging. (Jacob Grimm)

In language today we have lost the static quality of the ancient tongues. The sentence has become dynamic; every word and every sentence
speeds on to the next. The architecture of the
language is different: the vertical columns have
been laid low and the sentence is determined by
the impulse of the horizontal onward drive. "The
vertical columns would hold up the universal
flight like a barrier—but everything now moves
horizontally, in the line of flight." (*The Flight
from God*). The sentence becomes fluid and
dynamic. The words jostle each other in their
violent onward drive. Language today is sharp
and aggressive and there is often more aggressiveness in the very form of the language than

in the content it is expressing. Language is too self-conscious: each word comes more from the preceding word than from the silence and moves on more to the next word in front than to the silence.

3

In the ancient languages one notices that the birth of words from silence was not taken for granted but was considered an event of sufficient importance to require a pause in the flow of language before the arrival of the next word. Words were constantly being interrupted by silence. As a river being born receives at every moment waters from different springs, in like manner after every word a new spring of silence flowed into the stream of the sentence.

In the ancient languages the word was merely an interruption of the silence. Every word was rimmed around with silence. It was this surrounding rim of silence that gave it its individual shape, and kept it separate and distinct from all other words, fenced off from them with its individuality guarded by the silence. If there is no silence between words they lose their individual shape and personality. Instead of being persons they become an undifferentiated mass.

In the ancient languages there was a silence in the interval between two words. The language breathed silence, spoke silence, into the great silence from which it came.

In the classical style silence usually occupies an important space. Silence predominates in the style of Tacitus. Vulgar anger breaks out, the lower kind of anger chatters, but there is an indignation which feels the need of silence in order to leave the word to the things that are done in expectation of future justice. (Ernest Hello)

4

It is important that the ancient languages should be taught in schools because they reveal the origin of language in silence, the power of silence over language, and the healing influence of silence on language so much more clearly than these things are revealed today in our own language.

It is also important that through the ancient languages that are "useless", man should be redeemed from the world of mere profit and utility. We cannot "do much" with the ancient languages, but they bring us into touch with something that takes us beyond the world of pure expedience.

It is also important that dialects should be preserved. For a man who is in the habit of speaking dialect finds it impossible to move unchecked from word to word when he is writing or speaking the standard language. He always has to start out from the dialect to reach the standard written language at all. The standard language is not something ready-made that he takes for granted. When a man who usually speaks dialect speaks the standard language he drags the dialect underneath him like a brake-shoe under a cart. Dialect words are less easily manoeuverable. Like the silence that interrupts the flow of words and prevents language from becoming a mechanical routine, dialect, though to a lesser degree, protects the separate individuality of words.

Probably it is against the whole nature of language and therefore against the whole nature of man that dialects should be absorbed by the uniform standard language and that this should expand too far beyond its proper limits. In all human concerns there is a definite relationship between the quantity and the quality of a phenomenon. A human phenomenon cannot expand beyond a certain measure without destroying itself, and apparently this applies to language as to everything else.

> The finest truth of the English language is injured by its all-too-universal expansion. . . . Any bird lover must admit that the sparrow has many virtues but it must give him a nasty jerk to think of the powers of propagation of this small bird. If he thinks too hard he will become obsessed by the idea of a world from which all the more fastidious species have disappeared and only a universal sparrowdom remains. (Basil de Sélincourt)

THE EGO AND SILENCE

THE MAN whose nature is still possessed by silence moves out from the silence into the outside world. The silence is central in the man. In the world of silence, movement is not directly from one man to another but from the silence in one man to the silence in the other.

In the pictures of the old masters, people seem as though they had just come out of the opening in a wall; as if they had wriggled their way out with difficulty. They seem unsafe and hesitant because they have come out too far and still belong more to silence than to themselves. They stop and wait for another opening to appear in front of them through which they can get back again to the silence. It seems that in the silence the movements of these people meet before the people themselves meet. If you look at a group of these people together in a picture by one of the old masters—people who have each as it were just stepped out of the wall of silence—it is as though they were all gathered together in a waiting room, waiting for the great opening of silence to appear before them through which they can all disappear again.

The situation with people today is exactly opposite. The primary factor is movement for its own sake, movement that hits a definite target only by accident, movement that happens before it has been decided why it is happening, movement that is always ahead of man himself—so far ahead that he has to jump to catch up with it, to jump so far ahead of himself that he cannot help jumping into other people, and so making himself and other people nervous.

Even in the midst of the modern world of noise, the substance of silence is still occasionally present in men. In the very busy Via Torino in Milan, right in the middle of the city, I saw a man in an old suit that was more than merely a covering for his body: it was part of the man himself, it had suffered with him, it was like a brownish grazed skin. The man was not standing and was not walking: as he walked he stood still, and as he stood still he moved forward a little. His face was gentle and rosy, but from his forehead and cheeks, furrows crowded into his face. His eyes looked out high above everything they met, and yet they were waiting for something to come up to them from near at hand. The left arm was held close to the body, as if the body would not let go of the arm, and yet he held his hand stretched out slightly. I put a note into it, and then I did not know (for I dared not wait to find out) whether the hand went back to the man and whether he put the money in his pocket. Or did the hand move on out to another, seeking for another hand to which he could give money? This man was living in the centre between giving and taking, between distance and nearness, between old age and youth. He was living from the silent substance in the central place within, from the meeting place and focus within from which every movement proceeds outward.

A man in whom the substance of silence is still an active force carries the silence into every movement. His movements are therefore slow and measured. They do not jolt violently against each other; they are borne by the silence; they are simply the waves of silence. There is nothing vague and undefined about such a man, nothing vague about his language: the fact that his movement and his words are made individually distinct from one another by the intervening silence makes his whole personality clearer than if the silence were not there at all and the man and his words were all part of one continuous noise.

The nobility of such a man comes from his carrying the silence into the world. He is not paralyzed by the quietness in which he lives out his life, for the quietness is related to the silence and the silence extends the frontiers of his life.

Even unrest could not consume such a man, for it would merely be as it were an oscillation of the silence.

Where silence has ceased to be an active force, however,

> quietness is no use to man, for it paralyzes and consumes where there is no silence; therefore he must trudge along restlessly and an inevitable instability dogs every fresh beginning. (Görres)

2

Within the realm of creative silence the individual does not notice any opposition between himself and the community, for the individual and the community do not stand against each other, but both face the silence together. The difference between the individual and the community ceases to be important in face of the power of silence.

In the modern world the individual no longer faces silence, no longer faces the community, but faces only the universal noise. The individual stands between noise and silence. He is isolated from noise and isolated from silence. He is forlorn.

In a world in which silence is still an active force, solitude is not dependent on subjectivity, does not derive from subjectivity. Solitude stands before man as something objective, even the solitude within himself; it stands before him as the objective silence. The saints who followed the way of solitude did not find themselves, but the objective solitude of silence, of which their own inward solitude only seemed a small part. The saint took solitude upon himself as if it had come to him from another and he took it as a matter of course. Therefore solitude for the saints was not the result of great exertion like the "inward" solitude of today. On the contrary, it was a token of relationship with the great objective world of silence and with its objective solitude. Therefore the saints received more from the solitude than they could have received from their own inner solitude alone, for it was in fact not merely their *own* solitude: it was outside themselves and more than their own solitude could ever have been. Where solitude is merely a part of the inwardness of the isolated individual it consumes and diminishes the individual.

3

A man who still has the substance of silence within himself does not need to be always watching the movements of his inmost being, does not need consciously to order everything, since much is ordered without his conscious knowledge by the power of the substance of silence, which can modify the contradictions at war within. Such a man may possess qualities that are incompatible and yet avoid a crisis, for there is room for contradictions within the substance of silence.

Life is then not torn apart into the polarities of faith and knowledge, truth and beauty, life and spirit; the whole of reality appears before man, and not merely the conceptual polarities. Human life is not determined by the incompatible choices of Either-Or but by the mediation of the polarities. The substance of silence stands between the contradictions and prevents them from fighting each other. The one element in the contradiction must first travel over the broad, appeasing surface of silence before it can reach the other. The substance of silence mediates between the incompatible polarities.

It is only here that man is raised above his own inner contradictions, and only here that he has humour. For in the face of silence the contradictions lose their conspicuousness, are swallowed by the silence. To achieve a sense of humour,

> one must have the infinite cheerfulness and confidence which are necessary in order to rise above the contradictions of one's own personality and not to be unhappy and bitter about them. (Hegel)

If there is no substance of silence within, the contradictions are exposed to analysis and discussion. "Happiness and contentment" vanish and humour ceases.

Man is better able to endure things hostile to his own nature, things that use him up, if he has the silent substance within. That is why the peoples of the East, who are still filled with the substance of silence, endure life with machines better than the peoples of the West, whose silent substance has been almost completely destroyed. Technics in itself, life with machines, is not injurious unless the protective substance of silence is absent.

Unamuno says that Goethe did not develop all the possibilities that were in him. A sentence like that could only be said in a world that has lost all relationship with silence. It has been forgotten that the possibilities that are not fully realized nourish the substance of silence. Silence is strengthened by them and gives of this additional strength to the other potentialities that are fully realized.

What falls into the substance of silence is the share that silence has in the things of human life. That is still a part of silence. Sometimes in conversation a man holds something back inside himself, he does not allow it to come out in words; it is as though he feels he must keep back something that really belongs to silence.

It often happens that a whole nation may not realize certain potentialities for a long period in its history. For instance, the gift of poetic creation may remain dormant. But the potentiality is not destroyed, it is simply not realized. It may be resting and recuperating in the silence. Yet there is beauty in such a silence, the beauty that comes from the all-permeating silence of un-written poetry.

There is no silent substance in the world to-day. All things are present all the time in an at-mosphere of noisy rebelliousness, and man, who has lost the silence in which to sink the all-too-many, all-too-present multitude of things, allows them to evaporate and vanish in the all-consum-ing emptiness of language.

The silent substance that relieves man of the oppressiveness of things is lacking in the world today. In order to relieve him of the burden in another way, the attempt is made to classify the individual and bring him into touch only with those things that suit his mental constitution.

This is the new method in education. Do not teach the child anything that does not suit its par-ticular mental constitution. But in a world where the substance of silence is known to be still ac-tive, there is no danger in teaching a child things not immediately congenial to its particular tem-perament. The child can be allowed to expand beyond the structure of its own mind into the realm of, for example, Latin and Greek, for which it may not seem to have any aptitude. The silent substance in the child assimilates the for-eign material, fuses it with the other contents of the mind, broadens the whole nature of the child, and extends its mental frontiers. Proper education and proper teaching are based on the substance of silence.

We have said above that the man who lacks the substance of silence is oppressed by the all-too-many things that crowd in upon him every moment of his life today. He cannot be indifferent to the fact that new things are being presented to him every moment, since he must somehow enter into relationship with them. There must be an emotional reaction to each new object so that he can respond, and it is part of the nature of man that he should respond to the object before him. When too many objects crowd in upon him and he has within no silent substance into which a part at least of the multitude of objects can disappear, the resources of emotion and passion which he has at his disposal are insufficient to meet and respond to all the objects. The objects then lie all around him menacingly and without a proper home. To save man from this invasion and congestion of the too-many objects that are beyond his powers of assimilation, he must be brought into relationship again with the world of silence, in which the many objects find their true order automatically, in this world of silence where they spread themselves out into a balanced unity.

When the substance of silence is present in a man, all his qualities are centered in it; they are all connected primarily with the silence and only secondarily with each other. Therefore it is not so easy for the defect of one quality to infect all the others, since it is kept in its place by the silence. But if there is no silence, a man can be totally infected by a single defect so that he ceases to be a man and becomes so entirely identified with the defective quality that it is as though the defect and the evil it represents were covered merely by a human mask.

The silent substance is also the place where a man is re-created. It is true that the spirit is the cause of the re-creation, but the re-creation cannot be realized without the silence, for man is unable wholly to free himself from all that is past unless he can place the silence between the past and the new.

Today, with the lack of silence, man cannot be re-created; he can only develop. That is why so much value is set on "development" today. But "development" takes place not in silence but in the to-and-fro of discussion.

The substance of silence is necessary for re-creation, and it is also necessary for happiness. Happiness, which comes down to man from the realm of mystery, is glad to find its way into the breadth of silence. There is an immeasurability in happiness that only feels at home in the breadth of silence. Happiness and silence belong together just as do profit and noise.

Where the resources of silence have been exhausted, everything about a man is calculated in terms of profitability. Profitability and loudness give a man a right to possessions and office today. But in a world where silence was still present far and wide, Cicero said in a speech for Pompeius that he ought to be given the supreme command in the war against pirates not only because he had proved himself a good soldier but above all because good fortune was with him.

Grief and silence also belong together. Grief achieves a poise in the breadth of silence. The force of the passions is lost, and grief, purged of passion, appears all the more clearly as pure grief. The lamentation in grief is transformed into the lamentation of silence. On the river of tears man travels back into silence.

KNOWLEDGE AND SILENCE

I

"THE HUMAN mind not only perceives the object as it is presented to the mind, but there is a movement in the mind which goes out beyond the object" (Husserl). There are more possibilities in the movement of the mind than are required for the mere perception of the object. They give breadth to the mind.

The breadth of the mind and the breadth of silence belong together, for the breadth of the mind needs a corresponding natural breadth exterior to itself. It is true that the mind is autonomous and can create its own breadth for itself, but the breadth of silence acts as a kind of natural reminder. When the human eye comes from the breadth of silence, it does not concentrate merely on one specific part of a phenomenon. It is true that the All-Comprehending Being of God is the background from which the mind receives its own reflected power of all-embracing knowledge, but in the world of immanence, silence is the impulse that gives its all-embracing quality to the human eye. What is seen is then not merely one aspect—the purely economic, the psychological, or the racial aspect —but the whole of the phenomenon.

When the eye concentrates on but a single aspect, it tries to compensate itself by artificially enlarging that aspect, making it absolute (be it the economic, the psychological, or the racial). By this quantitative expansion of the phenomenon a pseudo breadth is achieved which is a sign of the human desire for the All-Comprehending, for the whole.

It is not long before the eye sees the particular part only when it is conspicuous, when it is clearly opposed to another part, when it juts out sharply from the other parts. Opposites are conspicuous and strike the eye more easily than the whole reality of a thing, for that is inconspicuous. We have for example become unable to see the whole reality of faith and of knowledge; of all these things we know only the contradictions and the polarities. "Life and spirit", "faith and knowledge", are regarded as valid only when they are in polar opposition to each other. Man is no longer able to give enough room to life and spirit, faith and knowledge, so that each man can exist satisfactorily without impeding the other.

There are not anything like so many polarities as it might appear. What happens is that phenomena are especially manipulated so as to seem a contradiction to other phenomena, since otherwise they may fail to catch the eye. Unless they are presented to the eye in this especially prepared form the eye will simply not see them at all.

For example: there is a real opposition today between America and Russia. But the Americans and the Russians—and not only they—exaggerate the differences between them, make them overdistinct, because today people do in fact see nothing but the differences between things, the conspicuous and sensational differences that have to be exaggerated in order to be perceived at all. The unobtrusive things of life are ignored today; they might as well not exist. From this exaggeration of the differences a war might well arise. That would be the most terrible thing imaginable: if war were to come not from passion or political necessity but merely from a psychological defect in man, which forces him to exaggerate the differences between phenomena in order to notice they are there at all.

2

When a man is in relation with silence, he is not burdened by his knowledge. Silence takes the burden from him. Men of earlier days were not oppressed by their weight of knowledge, however heavy it may have been: silence helped to carry weight. The knowledge was not pent up. The excess of knowledge disappeared into the silence so that man was able to face things with ever renewed innocence and lack of prejudice.

Silence was woven into the very texture of the whole approach to knowledge; there was no urge to unveil everything. Silence was allowed to have its share in things by keeping many things inviolate from contact with language.

In that world of silence things were not so conspicuous as they are today (where they seem to be calling out, appealing to man to take them on and concern himself with them exclusively). Things seemed to belong more to silence than to man, which is why he did not lay such violent hands on them, did not exploit them so intensively for his own ends; and even the results of inquiry and research pointed rather to the silence behind than to the thing itself. What was discovered seemed to be nothing but silence made audible. It was simply the part of silence which had of its own accord revealed itself to man.

Knowledge was not torn out of silence; it was still in relationship with silence. It was, as it were, prepared with the ingredients of silence and therefore still belonged to silence. For example, knowledge in the world of Herodotus is very various and variegated, but all the same there is a peace over all the mass of knowledge —the peace which comes from the calm gaze of the gods, which is sent on in advance in order to accompany into the silence of the gods that in things which belongs to the gods.

Just as there is no difference today between silence and language (silence is no longer a phenomenon on its own, but merely the word that has not yet been spoken), so there is today no longer any difference between what has and what has not yet been investigated. What has not yet been investigated, what is still hidden and mysterious, is no longer a phenomenon in itself but simply that which has not yet been investigated.

That does not mean that modern science is useless, but it does mean that in science today there is no real meeting between man and the object of his investigation. That is the fundamental defect in the whole feverish activity of science today: there is no longer any need for a personal meeting, a personal encounter with the object. The object and the investigator are in fact of little significance. They have been depersonalized by the methods of modern science. The whole process has been mechanized. Formerly the encounter between man and the object was an event: it was like a dialogue between man and the object under investigation. The object was given into man's care and keeping, and through the personal meeting with man the object became *more* and man became *more* because through the meeting he had helped the object to become more than it was before the meeting. It was like that in the beginnings of modern science, in the days of Galileo, Kepler, Swammerdam.

THINGS AND SILENCE

I

WE HAVE SAID, in the first chapter, that silence belongs absolutely to the world of being, that it is characterized by pure being. The ontological power of silence enters into the things that are in silence. The ontic in things is strengthened by silence; the exploitable in things is far from the world of silence. It is no match for silence; it can do nothing against silence.

Being and silence belong together. Ages no longer related to silence, like the modern age, do not bother about the ontic in things. They are concerned only with the profitability, the exploitability, and the revolutionary possibilities in things.

The older peoples in which a man *was* more and *became* less, had a more childlike and a more modest and humble sense of the gifts of heaven. (Jean Paul)

The whole of a thing is in its being, but only a small part of the total being of a thing is taken up into its becoming, and the word that describes becoming only approaches the reality of a thing in so far as parts of the being of a thing are in the becoming. "Being is related to becoming, as truth is to fancy" (Plato, *Timaeus*). True, it seems today that Existentialism is concerned with being, but it is not real being, but only parts, attributes of being, such as dread, care, death, insecurity—with which it is concerned; and these are artificially enlarged, made into absolutes, so that in fact they swallow up real being altogether.

2

Every object has a hidden fund of reality that comes from a deeper source than the word that designates the object. Man can meet this hidden fund of reality only with silence. The first time he sees an object, man is silent of his own accord. With his silence, man comes into relationship with the reality in the object which is there before ever language gives it a name. Silence is his tribute of honour to the object.

This hidden fund of reality cannot be taken up into human language.

À une certaine hauteur, dit Ernest Hello, le contemplateur ne peut plus dire, ce qu'il voit, non parceque son objet fait défaut à sa parole, mais parceque la parole fait défaut à son objet, et le silence du contemplateur devient l'ombre substantielle des choses qu'il ne dit pas. . . . Leur parole, ajoute ce grand écrivain, est un voyage qu'ils font

par charité chez les autres hommes. Mais le silence
est leur patrie. (Léon Bloy, *Le Déséspéré*)

Man does not lose anything because he cannot
express this hidden fund of reality in words.
Through this literally unspeakable fund of reality
man is brought into relationship with the original
state of things before the advent of language, and
that is important. Furthermore, this hidden fund
of reality is a sign that things are not created
and not combined by man himself. If things
were due to man's creation, he would know them
absolutely in language.

In a world in which silence is still an active
force, a thing is related more with silence than
with other things. It stands on its own, belongs
to itself more than in the world without silence,
where things are interconnected but no longer
in relation to silence. In the world of silence a
thing offers its being to man directly; it stands
immediately before him as though it had just
been brought by a special act out of the silence.
It stands out clearly against the background of
silence. There is no need to add anything to it
to make it clear.

3

The eye that comes from the broad surface of
silence sees the whole, and not merely the parts,
because it sees with the broad, all-embracing

gaze of silence itself. The word that comes out of silence embraces the object with the original power that it receives from silence, and the object adds something of this power to its own substance.

When the word has lost its original relationship with silence it becomes pure sound and can touch only the surface of the object; it merely adds a label to the object. These word-sounds and word-labels then lead a life of their own amongst themselves as though the things they purport to describe did not exist at all. The things also lead a life of their own, thing with thing; for, when the word has been destroyed by separation from silence, it is no longer able to contain the thing it describes, and the thing becomes detached from the word. It loses all proportion and exceeds its own natural limits. Thing begins to produce thing (as in the world of today), as if man no longer existed at all. No thing seems newly created any longer—not even new things, since all things are like a mere particle in an everlasting succession of things. Therefore every thing seems boring and superfluous.

Things themselves turn away from man. The old statues of the gods in a museum, for example: they stand there sometimes as though they were conspiring against man. They stand detached like a white wall with nothing to say to man. That is the uncanny and the satanical thing about this detached world of things: it impresses man merely by its size and mass. But pure, detached factuality is fatal. It erodes and destroys the world's resources.

Two menacing structures face each other to-day: the non-world of verbal machinery, which is out to dissolve everything into the noise of words, and the non-world of mechanized things, which, detached from language, is waiting only for a loud explosion to create a language of its own. Just as a mute sometimes cries so loud that he seems to be tearing his own flesh in an attempt to achieve the power of speech, so things crack and explode today as though they were trying to burst forth into sound—the sound of doom.

HISTORY AND SILENCE

I

THERE IS a periodical quietness in the flow of
human history, in the history of individuals and
of nations, in which nothing of "historical" significance occurs at all.

Everything external is absorbed by the inward
silence of such periods. It is as though the outward events were trying not to disturb the placid
flow of silence, as though the world of silence
were being fed by the stillness of events. There
are eventless periods in human history, periods
in which history seems to carry silence—nothing
but silence—around with her; periods in which
men and events are hidden beneath the silence.
Perhaps the period from the fall of the Roman
Empire to the beginning of the Middle Ages is
an example of such a period of silence.

Perhaps the reason there is so little recorded
history in the early ages of mankind's evolution
is that silence was still such a power in human
life—the silence from which all historical events
came and to which they returned. There was
no "history", only silence. The "historical" personalities and events were only positions from
which silence gazed at man. From the silence

of these "historical" personalities and events man
learnt his own silence.

History lives in two different modes—that of
the clearly visible daylight and that of the dark
invisible silence.

Many events not remembered and recorded by
history are not therefore, as Hegel imagined,
"without justification"; they are rather events
known only to silence.

It is wrong to say that it is a defect in man
that his powers of observation and memory are
insufficient to take in and remember the all-too-
many events of history. Man was not intended to
notice and remember everything that happens.
History does not belong to man alone, but also
to the invisible silence.

Silence is always close to history. There was
an example of this at the end of the last World
War, the war that was like a rebellion of noise
against silence; when silence was powerfully
present at least for a few days. Nothing was said
about the war; it was absorbed by the silence
before it was spoken. Silence was for a time
more potent than all the horrors of the war.
It could have been a healing influence, and the
world could have been transformed and re-
created in that silence if it had not been overrun
and destroyed by the noise of the whole indus-
trial machine getting down to work again. That

was the great defeat that mankind suffered immediately after the war.

We have said that silence is as much a part of history as noise; the invisible as much a part of history as the visible. But roughly since the French Revolution man has taken note only of the loud facts of history. He has overlooked the things of silence which are just as important. It is pure materialism to regard only the audible facts of history as important.

It is true that historical persons and historical events reach up into the realm of the visible and the audible, but they also penetrate deep down into silence: they are projections from the ground of silence. Historical events and personalities not only bring their actions to man, they also bring the silent ground of history. They are like draught-animals drawing silence on behind them.

The silent side of history is seen a little in the silent suffering of men and nations. But more suffering is lived through than is seen from the outside. It seems that mankind prefers to suffer in silence, prefers to live in the world of silence, even if it be by suffering, than to take its suffering into the loud places of history. This is the only possible explanation of the patient endurance shown by whole nations under the heel of tyranny.

In the midst of the loudness of history these

suffering nations are ambassadors from the world of silence, allies of the world of silence. It seems that such great suffering can be imposed on these people only because the great silence that is in the world helps the silence that is in man himself to bear the burden of suffering. Suffering becomes unbearable only when, separated from the great silence in the world, it is merely a part of the noise of history, and then has to bear its burden alone.

2

From time to time, as we have said already, there are periods in history in which the silence is more evident than the noise. History does not flow in a straight line from the noise of one age to the noise of the next. The flow of noise is sometimes interrupted by an age of silence. In fact, silence can move into an intrinsically noisy age and fill it with something of its stillness. Today, however, it is the reverse that happens. It is noise and loudness that invade the silent places of history.

There are nations that seem to slumber in silence for long centuries: such are the Spaniards during the last three hundred years. The silence in which they live is not an emptiness, nor is it a symptom of sterility. It is rather a sign of the importance and high value of silence for the

Spaniards. Spain has been considered backward
and old-fashioned because it did not join in the
universal noise and mobility of the modern age
by industrializing its economy. But Spain is no
more backward than a child that wants to stay
with its mother, or that comes back to its mother,
and to silence.

In the silent substance of such nations as Spain
there is a great reserve of help and strength for all
the other nations. All of us, the nations of the
modern world of noise, live on the capital of
silence which lives on in the life of a people like
the Spaniards. Such nations are passive, slumbering and silent not only for themselves but for the
other nations, for the noisy and the wide-awake
as well. Spain and many of the peoples of Asia
and Africa have silence in safe keeping not only
for themselves but for the rest of us as well.
We should all be much more ravaged by the
evils of this all-too-wide-awake world of noise if
we could not share in this surviving fund of
silence. All the nations of the world belong to
each other. That is why we can draw on the
silence of other nations just as they can draw on
our wide-awake alertness.

3

In the ages when silence was a more active influence than noise, much importance was at-
tributed to omens: the silent flight of birds, the

silent figurations of immolated animals, the silent motions of nature.

> When Galba rode to Rome a few days before his death and everywhere along the road victims were being slaughtered, a bull which had been enraged by the blow of the axe, tore itself loose, ran up to the emperor's chariot and covered him over and over with blood. Shortly after Galba was murdered. (Suetonius)

The inward substance of man was still replete with silence. That is why the silence in the world outside man, in the silent omens, in the silent flight of birds and the quiet motions of nature, could easily move into the human world; and it was so much at home there that it completely failed to notice the moment of its arrival.

The world of the word by and through which man exists, the world of the Christian, can be endangered by this world of omens. It was therefore banished into the silence by the Word of Christ.

Where the Word speaks, omens have no further need to speak, do not dare to speak. But when language is no longer firm and clear, as in our own world today, man goes out again in search of omens. But the omens of today no longer point to a reality: they only show the destruction of language. They are there only because of its destruction. To be sure, the destruction of the word is itself an omen, but it is an omen only in the sense that a ghost is an omen.

In other words, it points not to a future but to a past reality, to the ruins of the word.

What men regard as an omen today is like the statue of an ancient god, an imitation made of plaster of Paris and crumbling at man's first sight of it.

4

When man is no longer under the direction of silence nor of the word, history and events themselves undertake to teach him. Truth that can no longer reach man through the word is made clear by historical events. The Word of Christ had warned man against turning to evil, but as the word fell on deaf ears events were sent to teach him. The ruin against which man had refused to be warned in time by the *word*, was now revealed to man through the *fact* of the ruin of his own existence. Truth spoke not through words but through the events of war and other terrors.

As men no longer believed in the *teaching* that violence and hatred and crime should not hold sway among them, it was brought home to them by the *fact of war*. (*Hitler in Ourselves*)

In the life of Christ, history itself, sacred history, spoke the word. God Himself came into the word, the word that man had forsaken.

WORLD OF MYTH

THE WORLD of myth lies between the world of silence and the world of language. Like figures that seem to loom larger than life in the gathering twilight, the figures of the world of myth seem huge as they emerge from the twilight of silence.

Their language is not that of words but of deeds writ large on the wall of silence. The words they speak when their deeds are done seem to be especially planned, as if in expectation of the coming of man.

Christ came so directly from silence into the word (this directness of Christ also gave human words their greatest directness) that the whole world *between* silence and language—the world of mythology—was exploded and bereft of its significance and value. The characters in the world of myth now became demons stealing language from man and using it to cast demonic spells. Until the birth of Christ they were the leaders of men, but now they became the misleaders, the seducers, of men.

Before the coming of Christ, in the final centuries before His birth, a silence went through the ancient world. The old gods were silent, actively silent as an offering to Christ, the God who was coming to men. Now that men no longer sacrificed to the old gods, the gods themselves offered their silence as a sacrifice to the new God. They offered it that He might transform it into the Word.

IMAGES AND SILENCE

IMAGES ARE silent, but they speak in silence. They are a silent language. They are a station on the way from silence to language. They stand on the frontier where silence and language face each other closer than anywhere else, but the tension between them is resolved by beauty.

Images and pictures remind man of life before the coming of language; they move him with a yearning for that life. But pure aestheticism, the exclusive love of pictures, is a danger to the true nature of man, if he is tempted to yield to the pressure of this yearning and to surrender language, which is his true nature. The very beauty of images and pictures only increases the danger.

It is the soul that preserves the silent images of things. The soul does not, like the mind, express itself about things through the medium of words, but rather through the images of things. Things have a dual existence in man: first in the soul through images, then in the mind through words.

The images of things are preserved in the soul as before the creation of language.

The images in the soul point to a higher realm

beyond language, where there is nothing but images, where images speak as words and words as images.

> The difference between our active thinking and the thinking of God is that God expresses Himself through things themselves, using them as a language, whereas we express our thoughts only in the language of words. (Solger)

It may be that things bring their images to the soul so that the soul may pass them on to the Divine, to the Original of all images and all things.

Too many things crowd in on man today, too many images press in upon his soul. There is no more silent peace in the soul, only a silent lack of peace. Man becomes nervous and confused because the images whose real nature it is to create peace in the soul bring him an uneasy lack of peace instead. The images no longer give the peace of their own silence to the soul; they take peace from the soul by disturbing and consuming it with their riotous jostling one with another.

Silence has been banished from the world today. All that is left is muteness and emptiness. Silence seems to survive only as a mere "structural fault" in the everlasting flow of noise. It is therefore all the more important that the silent images should be preserved in the soul.

We have said that things have a dual existence
in man, first as images in the soul, then as words
in the mind. The silent images of things in the
soul and the words about things in the mind co-
exist in man. The silent images of things in the
soul bring their silence to the words that are
the life of the mind. They work silence into the
texture of language; they keep it supplied with
silence, with the original power of silence.

The more clearly the images of things are
present in the soul, the more surely will the soul
preserve words from the perils of unbridled
freedom. For there is a centripetal force in
images, which holds the parts of an image together by the power of the idea of the image,
so that the image rests in itself, is centered in
itself. Words that are still in relationship with
images have part in this centripetal force and are
thus preserved from the dangers of a sudden
violent explosion. For the figurative word, the
word related to an image, is less expansive than
the abstract word, and it protects man from the
dangers of the unrestrained association of ideas.

Past, present, and future are in a unity in
silence. This unity is also present in the soul,
in the silent images of the soul, but it is not
there as the knowledge of past and present—such
knowledge is the province of the mind. Unity
is present in the soul as a premonition of past,
present, future. There is a premonition in the

silent images of the soul. The word has knowledge but the image has premonitions. And when it is close to the images of the soul, even the word begins to share them.

The word does not then become vague and indefinite; rather it gains in definition and clarity. The nearness of the image makes the thing it describes clearly visible to the word. The image protects the word from the infiltration of something that does not really belong to the word.

Dreams are also images filled with silence. They are like gaily coloured transfer pictures on the surface of silence. It may be that dreams bring silence back to the man who has used up all too much of it in the daytime.

When the images of dreams fade away, the dew of silence that remains flows down softly into the troubles of a new day.

The images in dreams are more violent than the images in the soul. That is why past, present and future are more violently confused in dreams; and why some dreams are so prophetic.

Psychoanalysis destroys the essential nature of dreams; it destroys their silent power by delivering them over to the noisy altercation of analysis. The psychoanalytical analysis of dreams is the occupation of the silent world of dreams by noise.

LOVE AND SILENCE

THERE IS more silence than language in love.

Aphrodite, the goddess of love, came out of the sea, the sea of silence. Aphrodite is also the goddess of the moon, which catches the silence of night in the net of the golden threads it lowers to the earth.

The words of lovers increase the silence. They only serve to make the silence audible. Only love can increase the silence by speaking. All other phenomena take something from silence; only love gives of its own self to silence.

Lovers are the conspirators of silence. When a man speaks to his beloved, she listens more to the silence than to the spoken words of her lover. "Be silent", she seems to whisper. "Be silent that I may hear thee!"

Past, present, future, are in a unity in silence. Lovers are therefore raised above the relentless continuity of time. Everything can begin again. The future and the past are both enclosed in the eternal present. Time stands still for lovers. The clairvoyance and premonitions of lovers come from the unity in which past, present, and future are present in love.

Nothing interrupts the normal flow of ordinary life so much as love. Nothing takes the world back into silence more than love.

Through the silence that is in love, language is taken out of the world of verbal noise and bustle and led back to its origin in silence. Lovers are close to the beginning of all things, when language was still uncreated, when language could emerge at any moment from the creative fullness of silence.

Not only language but lovers themselves are redeemed by love from the world "of derived phenomena" (Goethe), and led to the primary underived phenomena. Love itself is a primary phenomenon and that is why lovers are solitary among other men. For they live in the world of primary phenomena, in a world where the static is more important than the dynamic, the symbol more important than the explanation, silence more important than speech.

The reticence that is in love is the reticence that is in all beginnings. Lovers hesitate to move away into the noisy bustle of the world from the world of beginnings in which they dwell in love.

All the transformation that a man or a woman can undergo in the experience of love comes from that new beginning that is the gift of all primary, underived phenomena. And the strength they receive from love comes from the power that love enjoys as one of the primary phenomena.

The faces of lovers shine with the radiance of the original light of love. That is why faces become more beautiful in love.

All the mystery of lovers comes from the nearness of the mysterious origins of love. The closer they live to this original mystery the firmer and the more enduring will be their love.

Lovers are restless, it is true. But it is the restlessness of the mystery of love shrinking back from appearing in reality, trembling as it hovers on the brink of the external world.

Yet it yearns for self-realization, and no other primary phenomenon ventures out so far into the world of the external as love. In no other outward reality is a primary phenomenon so clearly visible as in the outward reality of love. Nowhere else are the original mystery and the outward reality so near to each other as in love.

We have said there is more silence than language in love. The fullness of silence that is in love reaches to the silence that is in death: love and death belong together. Every thought and every deed in love reaches out through silence to death. But the miracle of love is that where death might be, the beloved appears.

In love there is more silence than speech.

It is incomparably easier to love when one is silent than when one speaks. The seeking after words is harmful to the motions of the heart in love. If in

life one loses nothing but love the loss is great, if
one knows the true value of love. (Hamon, quoted
in Brémond, *Mysticism and Poetry*)

It is easier to love when silent. It is easier because in the silence love can reach out into the
remotest corners of space. But there is also a
danger in this silence: this space ranging out
into the remotest corners is unrestrained and un-
controlled; there is room in it for everything,
even for the things that do not belong to love.

It is language that first makes love clear and
well-defined, that gives it only what belongs to
it. It is language that first makes love concrete
and sets it firmly on the solid ground of truth.
Only through language can love become the true
love of man and woman.

Love is a simple spring which has left its flower-
surrounded bed of pebbles and which now as
stream or river changes its nature and appearance
with every wave and finally pours itself out into an
immeasurable ocean, which seems to be full of
monotony to imperfectly developed minds but on
the shores of which the great souls become absorbed in infinite contemplation. (Balzac)

SILENCE AND THE HUMAN FACE

I

THE HUMAN FACE is the ultimate frontier between silence and speech. It is the wall from which language arises.

Silence is like one of the organs of the human face. Not only the eyes and mouth and brow are in the human face, but silence is there as well. It is everywhere in the face; it is the foundation of every part.

The cheeks are the walls that cover up the word from the sides. But the violent motion of the lines of the nose shows that what is held together between the surfaces of the cheeks wants to get outside.

From the vault of the brow silence does not strive outward; it trickles inwardly like dew.

From the two openings of the eyes comes light instead of language, light that brings brightness into the gathering of silence in the face. If it were not so, the silence would be dark.

When the mouth speaks it is as if not the mouth itself but the silence behind it were pressing it into speech. The silence is so full that it would drive the face upwards if it could not

relax and release itself in language. It is as though silence itself were whispering words to the mouth. Silence listens to itself when the mouth is speaking.

In silence the lines of the mouth are like the closed wings of a butterfly. When the word starts moving, the wings open and the butterfly flies away.

This extraordinary act of the creation of speech from silence occurs unnoticed and undramatically in the face. Therefore there is a calm in the face. All its movements are calm, for nothing can be important any longer now that the greatest event, the creation of the word, proceeds so calmly. It is very mysterious that silence is not diminished by the word that comes from silence, but that its density is increased thereby and that the word itself is increased by the greater density of the silence.

The power of silence was once so great in the human face that all external happenings were absorbed by this silence. The resources of the world were thereby as it were unspent and unexhausted.

2

If man had no language he would be nothing but an image and a symbol and identical with his own image, like the animal that is exactly as it looks. The animal's appearance is its nature, its image is its word. If man had no language then he and the creatures of the earth would be only images and symbols. The earth would be full of memorials; God would have set up creation only as it were as a memorial to Himself.

But man has language, and he is thereby more than an image and a memorial. He is master of his own image, for through the word he decides whether he will or will not accept what appears of his nature in the image, the outward appearance and form that he presents to the world, as himself. Through the word he is free to raise himself above his own image and external appearance, to become more than his image.

Man can be what he looks like but he does not need to: he can decide through language whether he wants to rise above the image of his face.

> When Zopyrus, who boasted that he could tell a man's character from his appearance, met Socrates and forecast the presence in Socrates of many vices, he was laughed to scorn—by all except Socrates himself. Socrates agreed with him: he, Socrates, had come into the world with those vices, but he had rid himself of them with the aid of reason. (Cicero)

Therein is the dignity of the human face: that it is where man decides whether he will accept what is expressed merely in the silent image of the face. Through this decision man is raised out of the merely natural flow of creation, and creates himself anew through the power of mind and spirit. Man does not need to be dependent on his external appearance: the word remains the final judge and master.

Man is determined more by language than by anything else. He is more related with language than with his physical body and the physical order of nature. The solitude around the human body is there because man has been lifted high above all the other physical phenomena of nature. Language watches over him and he belongs to language. But the transparency of the human figure comes from the relationship of man to language: the spirit that is in language makes the human figure transparent, loosens it so that the human form stands there as if it were not bound to the material body at all.

When man ceases to rise through language above what he seems to be—that is, above his purely external appearance, this external body is then separated from the word and becomes pure nature—but fallen, evil nature.

Perhaps man has broken out into the great barbarism of our time because having become now a purely animal nature after losing the order that is established by the spirit in language, he is trying to establish a connection between himself and the animal order.

Having fallen from the word, human nature is also no longer able to establish a connection

between itself and the order of extra-human nature. It lies in an abyss between the word that is
no longer present with it and the rest of nature
with which it cannot establish a connection.
Malignantly it lies between nature and the word.
In the place of the word it has mere shouting
and emptiness in the place of silence. "Man can
preserve his human form only so long as he
believes in God" (Dostoevsky)

3

The human form in itself, without the word,
the silent human form, is like a mere external
phenomenon; that is to say, it is as though it
appears in one moment only to vanish in the
next. Animals appear like that, too: like a picture in a dream belonging more to the evanescent
dream than to stable reality. Animals seem to
have dropped out of a human dream. Man is
always a little frightened at things that have
fallen out of his own dreams and then stand
staring at him as if they were completely foreign
to him.

Animals have a violent actuality. Nothing
makes its actual presence felt so violently as an
animal, and yet it is merely the actuality of a
passing moment. It is the same actuality of the
moment which is the quality of images in dreams.
(The snake has not even this actuality of the
moment. It is as it were always slithering through

holes, like a trickling stream between two holes, which is what makes it so sinister in contrast to other animals and in contrast to man. Birds, on the other hand, are not lacking in actuality. They fly quickly past, it is true, but the way of their flight is like an arch that returns again and again to its beginning.)

It is only through language that man becomes more than a mere physical phenomenon and breaks through the limitations of his own body. Through language he becomes firmly established: not a fleeting, transient animal, but a firm, enduring reality, held fast by language. The word takes man out of the state of pure momentary actuality of the animal into the state of the moment that endures. The word that is truth creates an enduring reality, and an enduring support not only for what it holds fast itself but for things outside itself as well.

The momentary actuality of the animal and the enduring reality of man are such absolutely different qualities that man could never have come straight out of animal in to human nature. A special act was necessary: the act of truth through the word—for man to receive his uniquely human nature.

When man loses the word in which lie truth and the power to create the enduring reality of human nature, he becomes animal-like, transient and fluid, and this produces more transience and fluidity. Man simply swims aimlessly about in an enormous, swiftly scurrying fluid, trying to move faster than the fluid.

4

The man who no longer rises, with the word, through the decision of the spirit, above the limitations of his own body, is identical with his appearance and his handwriting. One can tell the character of such a man from his face and his handwriting and from his psychological reactions. But the man who is known in this way is not the real man but the man whose stature has been diminished by separation from the real word. Physiognomy, graphology and psychology are reliable in their findings only in so far as they apply to this diminished man. By claiming to be anthropology they in fact give a kind of scientific standing to this reduced state of man. This anthropology has the dark, subterranean quality that is common to everything concerned with man reduced to the level of the animal.

It is not only the fault of the physiognomist, the graphologist and the psychologist, that man is judged and measured in this way. It is predominantly his own fault for not rising above the state of pure factuality in which he finds himself placed. The face of such men lacks the invisible centre to which the several parts move and from which they are ordered. Instead they stand incoherently in an already divided face, provoking the observer to divide it still further. It lies all uncovered and exposed, inviting examination. What is lacking above all in such a face is the silence which demands silence from and in fact creates silence in the observer.

In such a face the experiences it has undergone are all too deeply engraven, all too clearly evident, and all too obtrusive and important. There is no breadth of silence to balance out and absorb the lines that mark the face.

The fact that the deep lines etched by experience vanish in the silence points to the important revelation that there is another world beyond personal experience, where the subjective is not important: the world of the objective.

If there is no silence in the face, then the word is no longer covered by the silence, before it comes out of the mouth: all words are openly present in the face. And even when words are not actually being spoken there is no longer a true silence: it only means that the word-machine is taking a rest. Even when the mouth is closed, noises rush out not only from the mouth but from every part of the face. The whole face is nothing but a race between the various parts to see which can shout the loudest.

5

The landscape and the countryside influence the human body and the human face, but the silent power of the landscape needs the silence in the human face if it is to exert its influence. Landscape can shape the human face if it is to exert its influence. Landscape can shape the human face only through the medium of silence. The powers of the landscape are far-reaching and they need a wide approach—the wide approach of silence, through which they can travel into the human face and shape it creatively.

The silent landscape becomes a speaking silence in the human face. The mountain dweller has the image of the mountains firmly etched in his face. Towering rocks are the bones in such a face. Passes, hiding places, and mountain peaks are present in such a face, and the brightness of the eyes over the cheeks is like the brightness of the sky over the dark enfolded mountains.

Tokens of the sea are likewise clearly imaged in the faces of those who live by the sea. The raised parts of the face—the nose, mouth, and projections—are like frozen ships on the wide sea of the face.

> The swiftly gliding ship came near to the shore. Then Poseidon came near, struck it with the palm of his hand and behold: suddenly turned to stone, it lay firmly rooted on the ground of the sea. (Homer)

The eyes seem to gaze from the distance out over the frozen ships of their own face. Sometimes when the sea outside is calm as though its very depths are slumbering, sometimes the frozen ships attempt to move.—But suddenly two heavy ships travel outside over the real sea, and the ships of the face are frozen again as they were before.

The landscape has its own monument in the human face, and the human face seems to hover over its own landscape, raising itself above and beyond itself, saved from itself. The subjective is no longer accentuated and the objective in the human face becomes clearly visible. This is a sign that the human face does not belong only to itself.

It does not mean, however, that subjectivity is destroyed when the human face participates in the objective. The subjective is simply put in its proper place, like the signature of the painter in a medieval picture: a monogram consisting of the initials of the master's christian and surname half hidden in a corner of the picture.

If there is no silence in the face, the face then becomes in the true sense of the word urbanized, uprooted from the countryside, literally self-possessed, just as a city is more self-possessed, more wrapped up in itself than is the countryside.

The landscape cannot appear in such a face, but man may sometimes still have a "relationship"

with the countryside, may still have an inward
understanding of it. Such a face is then empty
of landscape but too much filled instead with
"inwardness". Or rather, there is no silence and
no landscape there to cover and protect the
"inwardness".

Today there are no sea and no mountains in the
face. The face no longer welcomes them, it thrusts
them out. There is no place for them in the face.
Everything is so pointed, that it seems as if the outside world has been shaken off, pushed away by
this sharp pointedness in the face. The trees have
been sawed down in the face, the mountains
shovelled away and the sea drained off—and the
great city has built itself into the emptiness of the
face. (*The Human Face*) (Picard)

ANIMALS AND SILENCE

THE NATURE of man is more apparent in language than in his external appearance. "Speak, that I may see thee!" said Socrates.

The nature of animals, on the other hand, is expressed completely in their appearance. An animal is exactly as it looks; it must be so. Man *can* be as he looks but he need not be, for he can rise above his outward appearance through the gift of language: he can be more than is outwardly apparent. Man becomes apparent in language, animals in the silence of their physical appearance.

This is the perfection of animals—that there is no discrepancy in them, as there is in man, between being and appearance, inward and outward nature. This perfect correspondence is what constitutes the innocence of animals. "So much time was spent on the inward nature of man that his 'surface' (appearance) had to be endowed more sparingly", said Goethe. The very colourful surface of some animals seems like an attempt to break through the silence by means of violent colour. The silence that could not give rise to language changed itself into the very violent colour.

If it is so, as Plato says, that animals arose from man (*Timaeus*) so that he, man, might arise—if it is so, then with the animal in man the dense silence of nature was also expelled from man so that the word might have room to be the word.

But animals remain near to man, and with them the dense silence that is in them.

In earlier times animals were more important to man than they are today. The silence of animals made human speech and human movement heavier and slower. Animals carry silence around with them on behalf of man. They carry not only the burden of things on their backs but also the burden of silence.

Animals are creatures that lead silence through the world of man and language and are always putting silence down in front of man. Many things that human words have upset are set at rest again by the silence of animals. Animals move through the world of words like a caravan of silence.

Animals are images of silence. They are animal-images of silence more than they are animals. As the starry images scan the silence of heaven, so the animal-images of earth scan the silence of the earth.

A whole world, that of nature and that of animals, is filled with silence. Nature and animals seem like protuberances of silence. The silence of animals and the silence of nature would not be so great and noble if it were merely a failure of language to materialize. Silence has been entrusted to the animals and to nature as something created for its own sake.

The silence of animals is different from the silence of men. The silence of men is transparent and bright because it confronts the word, releasing the word in every moment and receiving it back into itself again. It is a relaxed silence, touched by the word and touching the word.

The silence of men is like the night in northern lands illuminated by the light of day.

Animals have a heavy silence. Like a block of stone. Animals stride over the blocks of silence, trying to tear themselves away but always chained to them.

Silence is isolated in animals; therefore they are lonely.

It is as though the silence in animals were materially tangible. It makes its way right through the outside of the animal, and animals are unredeemed not only because they lack speech, but also because the silence itself is unredeemed: it is a hard, coagulated silence.

It is true that the raven croaks, the dog barks, and the lion roars. But animal voices are only chinks in the silence. It is as though the animal were trying to tear open the silence with the force of its body.

"A dog barks today exactly as it barked at the beginning of Creation", said Jacob Grimm. That is why the barking of dogs is so desperate, for it is the vain effort, since the beginning of creation until the present day, to split the silence open, and this attempt to break the silence of creation is always a moving thing to man.

The voices of the birds are not desperate like the voices of the other animals. Birds seem to throw the notes of their song like balls against the silence, as in a game; they seem to catch their own notes again as they fall back from the surface of silence.

TIME AND SILENCE

TIME IS interspersed with silence.

Silently one day moves onward to the next. Each day appears unnoticed as if God had just put it down out of His own quietness.

Silently the days move through the year. They move in the rhythm of silence: the content of the day is noisy, but the advent of the day is silent.

It is not so much the equal measure of the hours, which is the same in every day, which connects one day with another, but the equal measure of the silence with which each day is newly born.

The seasons move in silence through the changing year.

Spring does not come from winter; it comes from the silence from which winter came and summer and autumn.

One morning in spring the cherry tree stands full of blossom. The white blossoms seem not to have grown on the tree but to have fallen through the sieve of silence. No sound was heard; they glided gently along the silence and it was that that made them white.

The birds sang in the tree. It was as if the silence had shaken out the last sounds from itself. Birdsong is like the picked-up notes of silence.

Suddenly the green appears on the trees. As one tree stands green beside another, it is as if the green had passed silently from one tree to another, as words pass from one to another in a conversation.

Spring comes suddenly: man looks into the distance as if he could still see the harbinger who brought the spring in silence. In spring a man's eyes gaze into the distance.

The reality of spring is so gentle that it does not need to break through the solid walls of time with noise. It simply seeps through the chinks of time and suddenly appears.

Children playing on the square are the first to come through the chinks. Even before the blossoms they come along with their balls in the air and their marbles on the ground.

They suddenly appear not as from their parents' houses but as it were out of the chinks, along with spring. They throw their balls high up in the air; they shout aloud, these first harbingers of spring showing the way to the things of spring that follow on behind.

Behind all the sounds of spring is the silence of time. It is a wall throwing back the children's words like balls from the walls of the houses.

The blossoms on the trees make themselves so

light, as if they wanted to settle on the silence, unnoticed by the silence itself; to be carried into the next spring in the ever-moving circle of the seasons, just as birds settle down on ships to be carried farther on.

Then, quite suddenly, the summer arrives.

The air is hot with the violence of its invasion. As if they had burst out from a covering, the things of summer suddenly appear in their fullness. But no one heard the summer come. It too was brought in silence. The covering enclosing the fullness of summer burst open in the silence. No one heard a sound when time put the summer down with a violent thud. Everything happened silently.

But now summer has appeared, everything begins to sound: the animal voices are stronger, people throw up their words like balls; out of the gardens and taverns voices tumble as if the room inside were too narow for them. It is the triumph of the sounds of summer over silence.

Silence is now hidden in the forest. The forest is like a green tunnel leading from the noise of summer into the silence. And as one sometimes sees lights in a tunnel, so the deer of the forest flash like lights illuminating the silence.

Silence is now in a hiding place, but any moment it can come out and cover everything again. In the noon of a hot summer's day every sound of summer is absorbed by the all-possessing silence. It is sometimes as if the summer stands quite still. It stands so fast, as if it would never move again. Its image seems to be impressed on and to remain in the air.

Then after silence has taken a new breath the autumn comes.

Like birds clustering thick on the wires before their departure, the apples sit on the branches. Here and there when an apple falls to the ground there comes a moment of stillness. It is as if the silence had held out its hand to try and catch the apple.

The colours of the leaves and fruits become more vivid. It is almost as though, if one were to tear them, a sound would come out of them. The dark blue berries of the grapes are like the heads of crotchets. The song of the harvesters lies concentrated in the dark crotchet-heads of the berries.

Everything moves closer to speech in the autumn: the silence itself seems to sound in between the songs of the harvesters.

In winter silence is visible: the snow is silence become visible.

The space between heaven and earth is occupied by silence; heaven and earth are merely the edge of the snowy silence.

Snowflakes meet in the air and fall together on

to the earth, which is already white in the silence. Silence meeting silence.

People stand silent on the side of the street. Human language is covered by the snow of silence. What remains of man is his body standing in the snow like a milestone of silence. People stand still and silence moves between them.

Time is accompanied by silence, determined by silence. Its quietness comes from the silence that is enclosed within it. But the sound of measurable time, the rhythmic beat of time, is drowned by the silence.

Time is expanded by silence.

If silence is so preponderant in time that time is completely absorbed by it, then time stands still. There is then nothing but silence: the silence of eternity.

When there is no more silence left in time, then the noise of its as it were mechanically flowing movement becomes audible. Then there is no more time, only the impetus of its onward flow. Men and things are then as it were pushed on by the movement of time, taken up into its mechanical onward flow, no longer independent, but merely a constituent part of time itself. Men, things, and time compete against each other as in a race; as if they existed only as competitors in the race—"the race against time" and the race of time against men and things.

Without the silence that is in time, there would be no forgetting and no forgiving. Just as time itself enters into silence, so what happens in time enters also; and therefore man is led by the silence which is in time to forgetting and forgiving.

When time has been completely absorbed by silence, in Eternity, there can be nothing but the great forgetting and forgiving, for Eternity is permeated by the great silence into which everything that has ever happened falls and disappears.

It is true, the spirit stands above time and above the silence that is in time; it is the spirit that determines forgetting and forgiving. But it is easier for the spirit to forgive and to forget when it meets the silence in time: through the silence the spirit is reminded of Eternity, which is the great silence and forgiving.

CHILDHOOD, OLD AGE
AND SILENCE

THE CHILD

THE CHILD is like a little hill of silence. On this little hill of silence suddenly the word appears. The little hill becomes quite small when the first word of the child is spoken. It sinks beneath the pressure of the word as if by magic, and the word tries to make itself look important.

It is as though with the sound that comes from its mouth the child were knocking on the door of silence and silence were replying: Here I am, Silence, with a word for you.

The word has difficulty in coming up from the silence of the child. Just as the child is led by its mother, so, it seems, the word is led by silence to the edge of the child's mouth, and is held so firmly there by silence that it is as though each syllable had to detach itself separately from the silence. More silence than sound comes out through the words of children, more silence than real language.

The words a child speaks do not flow in a straight line, but in a curve, as if they wanted to fall back again into the silence. They make their slow journey from the child to other people, and when they arrive they hesitate a moment, to decide whether they should return to the silence or stay where they are. The child gazes after its word as it might watch its ball in the air, watching to see if it will come back again or not.

The child cannot replace by another word the word it has brought with difficulty out of the silence; it cannot put a pronoun in place of a noun. For each word is there as it were for the first time, and what is there for the first time, what is quite new, naturally has no wish to be replaced by something else.

A child never speaks of itself as "I", but it always says its name: "Andrew wants . . ." The child would think it were disappearing if it were to replace its own name by a pronoun— its own name that has just come up out of the silence with the word and is there as it were for the first time ever.

The child's language is poetic, for it is the language of the beginning of things, and therefore original and first-hand as the language of poets is original and first-hand. "The moon has got broken", says the child of the new moon. "We must take it to mother to mend it".

The child's language is melodious. The words hide and protect themselves in the melody—the words that have come shyly out of the silence. They almost disappear again in the silence. There is more melody than content in the words of the child.

It is as though silence were accumulating within the child as a reserve for the adult, for the noisy world of the child's later years as an adult. The adult who has preserved within himself not only something of the language of childhood but also something of its silence, too, has the power to make others happy.

The language of the child is silence transformed into sound. The language of the adult is sound that seeks for silence.

Children—the little hills of silence—are scattered about everywhere in the world of words, reminding men of the origin of speech. They are like a conspiracy against the all-too-dynamic world of the words of today. And sometimes it is as though they were not only a reminder of where the word comes from but also a warning as to where it might return: back into silence. But what better thing could happen to the corrupted word than to be brought back into these little hills of silence to become immersed therein? Then there would be only little hills of silence on the earth, and in them the word would try to sink itself deep down into the hills so that out of the depth of the silence the first, the original, word might be born again.

THE OLD PEOPLE

The Word climbs up slowly out of the silence in the child, and the words of old men and women are slow, too, as they return to the silence that is the end of life. Like a burden that has grown too heavy the word falls out of the mouth of the old, more down into the silence than out-wards to other men, for the old speak more to their own silence than to other men.

They move their words like heavy globules hither and thither between their lips. It is as though they were rolling them back in secret into the silence, as though before they leave the earth themselves, the old men and women were trying to give back to the silence the words they received from the silence almost unnoticed when they were children.

An old man and an old woman sitting beside each other in silence outside their home in the evening. . . . They and every word that comes from them and every action to which the word gives rise, are within the silence. They are not even listening any longer to hear what the silence is saying, for they have already become a part of the silence. Just as they led the cattle to water, they now lead the evening to the watering place of silence and wait till it is satisfied. Then they slowly rise and lead it back into the warming light of the house.

Even before they move into the silence of death, the old have something of that silence within them; their movements are slow, as though they were trying not to disturb the silence at the end of the journey. With their stick to help them they still walk hesitantly as if on a bridge without railings, from both sides of which not language any more, but death, rises up to meet them. They go to meet the silence of death with their own silence within. And the last word of the old is like a ship carrying them over from the silence of life into the silence of death.

SILENCE AND THE PEASANT

I

THE VILLAGE . . . Shyly the walls of the houses rise from the earth, first as if step by step and slowly, horizontally, and then a little upwards into the air, carefully, as though they were afraid to meet something that should not be touched.

The paths in the village lie there as if they had been cast off like old shoes. They are short, they disappear round the corners and suddenly stop. They are like the remains of a great road that is no longer there. Only the silence still goes over them, and behind it a few people silently following in the wake of the silence.

But from the little windows of the houses silence watches itself passing on the path below.

The people are slow, as though they were trying to move in the slow rhythm of the silence itself.

Two people stand by each other talking in the street in the morning. They look round carefully as if they were still being observed by the silence of the night. The words go backwards and forwards between them stealthily, as if they are seeing whether they can still speak after the silence of the night. They have been speaking for a long time already, but it is as though the silence were becoming still more dense as time goes on.

2

In the spring the first primrose and a catkin slip out unobtrusively through a chink in the silence, and then all the crocuses and tulips are there. They come so suddenly that one can almost hear them, but the sound is changed into colour: into the brilliant reds and yellows of the tulips.

The birds begin to sing. It is as if the silence of the air were being grazed by the wing of the bird: such is the origin of song.

In the summer the flowers in the peasants' gardens are as thick as fruit, like coloured milestones, signposts on the road of silence.

Sometimes on a summer's day the village is sunk in silence, as if sunk under the earth. The walls of the houses are the last remains above the earth, and the church tower stands high like a cry for help, like a cry turned into stone in the silence.

On such a summer's day the flowers in the gardens are different: the dark flowers are like seaweed on the bottom of the sea of silence, and the bright ones like reflected images of the stars on the ground of silence, or like glistening fish in the water of silence.

3

The cattle in the fields: they are the animals of silence. The broad surface of their backs. . . . It is as if they were carrying the silence there. Their eyes are like brown pebbles on the road of silence.

Two cows in a field moving along with a man beside them. . . . It is as if the man were pouring down the silence from the backs of the animals on to the fields; as if he were ploughing with the silence.

The moo of the cow is like a rent in the silence, like silence tearing itself to pieces.

The wide gestures of the men in the fields— they are re-sowing the silence that has been destroyed in the towns.

4

The life of the peasant is a life in silence. Words have wandered back into the silent movements of man. The movements of the peasant are like a long stretched-out word that has lost its sound on a long journey.

The peasant repeats the same motions every time he mows and sows and milks, in every kind of work. The motions he performs are as concrete an image as the house he lives in and as the trees on the field. All the noise of work is absorbed into the constant pattern of the same repeated movements, and the peasant's work is surrounded with silence. In no other vocation is the pattern of daily work so clearly visible and concrete as in that of the peasant.

The peasant moving along behind his horses and the plough. . . . All the fields of earth lie underneath this plough, under the tread of the horse and the peasant. The motions of the peasant, the horse and the plough are independent of language as if they had never set out from language; as if the peasant, before he left home for the fields, had never said: Now I am going into the field to plough;—in fact, as if no man had ever spoken of fields and horses and ploughing, for the movements of the peasant are become like the silent orbit of a star.

The movements of the peasant are so slow that it seems as though the stars were moving with him and as though peasant and stars were crossing each other's silent paths.

The plenteous grain falling into the opened earth from the hand of the peasant is like the abundance of stars in the milky way. Grain and stars both shine through the mist and the haze.

The peasant's life is like a constellation of silence in the vault of the human sky.

Because the whole of the peasant's life became a regular pattern, it stepped out of the circle of the rest of human life and is linked more with the patterns of nature and the patterns of the inner life than with those men who are outside the world of silence and the world of pattern.

Sometimes when a peasant moves with the plough and the oxen over the broad surface of the field, approaching ever nearer to the edge of the horizon where the sky touches the earth, it is as if the vault of the sky might in the next moment take up into itself the peasant, the plough, and the oxen, so that he might plough the soil of heaven as one of the constellations.

5

The peasant is a link in the sequence of the generations, backwards and forwards, so that the generations of the past are with him in their silence, and with their silence future unborn generations as well. The individual in every other walk of life is not only more obtrusive than the peasant, but also more intensely involved in the present, more detached from the past and the future and from their silence.

When peasants make a great noise on their festive occasions, it is as if they were trying to break out of the silence, which they can do successfully only by the use of force.

Look at the movements of peasants in the old Dutch paintings. The movements of their faces and limbs are like those of men who have just risen from silence, violently shaking off the

peace and silence, and trying out all kinds of
movement at once as if they wanted to know
all the things one can do with the face and
limbs in crying and laughing, the things they
have forgotten in the silence.

6

A peasant and his wife sitting in the evening
in front of their house, both in a long silence.
. . . Suddenly a word falls from the mouth of
one or other into the silence. But that is no interruption of the silence: it is as though the word
were simply knocking to see if silence were
still there—and then it goes away again. Or it
is like the last word proceeding from a man so
that silence should have full sway, the last word
that runs after all the others that have been before
and disappeared, a straggler belonging more to
silence than to language.

This silence of the peasant does not mean the
loss of language. On the contrary: in this state
of silence man returns to the beginning of time,
when he was waiting to receive the word from
silence. It is as if he had never yet possessed
the word; as if it were now to be given to him
for the first time. It is not man but silence out
of which the first word now appears again.

Man towering up from the level of earth:
that is like the word leaping up from the surface
of silence. But only the peasant still has this

level ground of silence within him today. The peasant, towering up from the level of the field, corresponds to the level ground of silence out of which the word of man arises.

MEN AND THINGS IN SILENCE

I

Nous nous taisions. Heureux ceux, heureux deux amis, qui s'aiment assez, qui veulent assez se plaire, qui se connaissent, *qui s'entendent assez,* qui sont assez parents, qui pensent et sentent assez de même assez ensemble en dedans, chacun séparément, assez les mêmes, chacun côte à côte, de marcher long-temps, longtemps, d'aller, de marcher silencieuse-ment le long des silencieuses routes. Heureux deux amis, qui s'aiment assez pour (savoir) se taire en-semble. Dans un pays qui sait se taire. Nous mon-tions. Nous nous taisions. Depuis longtemps nous nous taisions. (Péguy)

It is a blessing to have a common understanding not only about the meaning of things but also about the meaning of silence. Simply not to be talking is not the same as to be silent. Silence must be present within a man as a primary reality in its own right, not merely as the opposite of speech. This living in the primary silence adds another life to man, who is only man through the word: it adds the life in silence. It points him beyond the life that is in the word to a life beyond the word, and it points him beyond himself.

Often Platon Karatajev said the exact opposite of
what he had said earlier, and yet both the one and
the other were right. . . . When Pierre was sometimes taken aback by the deep meaning of his
words he asked Platon to repeat what he had said.
But Platon was unable to remember the words he
had spoken only a minute before. . . . Platon did
not and could not understand the meaning of the
individual words torn out of their context. Every
word and every action of Platon was the expression of an activity which he himself did not understand yet which constituted the whole of his life.
Platon's life was meaningless as a single individual
life and received its meaning only as part of the
whole life which he felt flowing ceaselessly around
him. His words and his deeds streamed from him
as directly as the fragrance from a flower. (Tolstoy, *War and Peace*)

That is a picture of man inside such a firm,
unchanging order that the word is no longer
used to release an action. The actions follow one
another unobtrusively, unnoticed by anyone.

With this Platon of Tolstoy there is no further need of words and therefore the word has
a freedom of its own. It is no longer directly
bound to the object and no longer to other
words, but nevertheless it is not completely un-
leashed: it hovers blessedly over objects and
actions. The words are connected and held together not by formal external logic but by the
blessedness of this freedom of their own. Therefore "there is no contradiction here", and a man

"can say the exact opposite of what he had said before and yet the one and the other were both right".

The words do not point to themselves nor to the things and actions they describe, but to the blessedness of the inward freedom. Such a man can speak and yet be silent; and he can be silent and yet speak. In fact the silence is made audible by the word, and the bliss that is usually only a feeling becomes as visible as a concrete object, visible in its transparency.

2

The little old towns of the past seem to lie in an opening of silence, still surrounded by silence at their extremities. It is as if the covering had been removed from silence at one place; as if silence were itself looking down on to the little town.

There is still a kind of numbness in the houses, a shock caused by the all too sudden eruption of the little town from the surface of silence.

Everything is very close together in the little town. Houses, streets, and squares are all packed tight as if ready for instant removal. It is as if it needed only a little jolt and everything would disappear again through the opening in the silence.

The streets are like bridges over the silence.

And the people walk so slowly up and down as
though they were afraid the ground was not
firm enough to hold them.

Only the cathedral is secure, like the solid
opening of a shaft down which the silence moves
to the still deeper silence below.

Contrast with that the big cities of the modern
world. It is as though silence had suddenly exploded and thrown everything into disorder and
confusion. The city has been destroyed by the
explosion of silence. It lies there like what is
left behind after an explosion, like the ruins of
silence.

The language spoken by men in cities does
not seem to belong to them any longer. It is a
mere part of the general noise, as if the words
were no longer formed by human lips but were
only a scream and a shriek coming from the
mechanism of the city.

It is said today that people need only go into
the country to reach the "quietness of nature"
and silence. But they do not meet the silence
there; on the contrary, they carry the noise of
the great towns and the noise of their own souls
out into the country with them.

That is the danger of the "Back to the Land"
movement: the noise that is at any rate concentrated in the big towns, locked up as in a prison,
is let loose on the countryside. To decentralize
the big towns is to decentralize the noise, to
distribute it all over the countryside.

3

Sometimes, when the wall of a house stands in the light of noon, it is as though the light were taking possession of the wall on behalf of silence. One can feel the approach of the silence of the noonday heat. The light lies firmly on the wall as a sign that the wall belongs to the silence.

The gate in the wall is shut; the windows are covered with curtains; the people inside the house are very quiet, as though they were lowering their heads at the approach of the silence.

The inside wall seems to expand through the silence pressing in on it.

Then suddenly a song lights up on the wall from inside. The notes are like bright balls thrown at the wall. And now it is as though the silence rises from the wall and climbs upward towards the sky, and the windows in the wall are like the steps of a ladder leading the silence and also the song into the sky above.

4

Sometimes there is a seat by the side of a road, with a cat resting on it. And beyond the cobble-stoned street there is nothing but a meadow from which a steep slope falls to the valley. The seat, the cat, the street, the meadow seem to hover between the sky above the earth at the

bottom of the slope. And here, here in these few
things rests silence itself. It is as if the silence
had gone out of the rest of the world and taken
these few things with it here to take its rest
in them.

The cat is as motionless as if it had previously
been one of those stone animals that wait eternally on cathedral walls: the animal of silence,
able to watch over silence itself.

These few things—the animal, the seat in the
sun, the cobbled street, the field—are all lifted
out of the routine of the world by silence.
Animal, seat, and earth have returned to the beginning where only silence was, before the creation of language. In the beginning they were thus
as they are now, and thus they shall be brought
to the end of the world.

The man looking at them would like to add
his own silence to these things of silence, so
that it might travel with them again from the
beginning of the world until their end.—But
then he expresses what he sees before him in
the word, and in the word he sees the silence
even more clearly than with his eye.

5

A great wall of stone, the great outside wall of
the theatre at Orange in Provence: it is silence
itself.

It is not the silence that arises by crushing out

the word; here the silence is not ground down by the stonework. Here it is from the very beginning in the stone, in the stone as the Greek gods are in the marble, where it is not as if man had fashioned them out of the marble but as if they themselves had appeared in the marble exactly as they are; as if they had travelled for a long time through the blocks of marble until they came to the end of the marble mountain. As out of a gate, out of the last gate of the marble mountain, the gods step out of the marble.

And exactly so is the silence in this wall. It seems to have travelled through all the stones of earth, until it has arrived at the last wall of stone here, and now it waits. Round gates have already broken out of the wall below and at the sides, as if everything were prepared for the silence to move out from here into the world.

If the wall were only one single stone, it would be like a memorial of silence—only a memorial. But as it is, made up of many small stones, these stones as they rise from the ground and stretch out in all their length and breadth are like the limbs of silence. The silence is alive; it is no mere memorial. The many stones are like the stone flesh of silence. One can feel the texture of silence in this great wall of stone.

It is as though the whole earth could be supplied with silence from this place; in fact as if a whole world of silence could be erected from this place: the groundwork consisting of silence, rivers conveying silence instead of water between their banks, and on their sides trees standing packed tightly together as the stones here in the wall.

The trees bear a bright radiance on their branches between their leaves, and the bright radiance between the leaves is like the fruits of silence.

NATURE AND SILENCE

I

THE SILENCE of nature is a conflicting silence from the human point of view. It is a blessed silence because it gives man an intuitive feeling of the great silence that was before the word and out of which everything arose. And it is oppressive at the same time because it puts man back into the state in which he was before the creation of language; before the creation of man. It is like a threat that the word might be taken away from him again into that original silence.

If man were nothing but a part of nature, then he would never be solitary. He would always be connected with everything through silence— but in a relationship that would concern only the natural side of his nature. Man is not, however, only a part of nature, but also spirit, and the spirit is solitary when man is connected with things only through silence, for the spirit needs to be connected with things through the word. Then the spirit ceases to be solitary in the neighbourhood of silent nature: it speaks and is still in the silence. In fact through the word it can create silence. That is the sign of the divine origin of the word that out of it can arise the absolutely other, that which is not contained in the external givenness of the word: the unexpected silence.

The relation with things through silence is a permanent relationship, but the connection through the word is tied to the moment. But it is the moment of truth which appears in the word, and that is the moment of Eternity.

We have said that the silence of nature is permanent; it is the air in which nature breathes. The motions of nature are the motions of silence. The alternation of the seasons is the rhythm of silence; the pattern of the changing seasons is covered by silence.

The silence of nature is the primary reality. The things of nature serve only to make the silence clearly visible. The things of nature are images of the silence, exhibiting not themselves so much as the silence, like signs pointing to the place where silence is.

2

Silence was there first, before things. It is as though the forest grew up slowly after it: the branches of the trees are like dark lines that have followed the movements of the silence; the leaves thickly cover the branches as if the silence wanted to conceal itself.

A bird sings in the forest. That is not a sound directed against the silence; it is the bright glance falling from the eye of silence itself on to the forest.

The forest grows ever larger, because the silence grows ever greater. The leaves must fall more thickly and the birds sing more loudly. But now the bright eye of silence can no longer penetrate the forest.

The broad back of the mountain. . . . Gently it presents itself to the human eye and waits patiently for man to cry. Then the forest catches up the word and gives it back to man in the echo, for it belongs to man and not to the forest.

After the echo the silence becomes still deeper, but where the echo moves along the mountain the ridge of the forest seems exalted.

Outside the forest, the flowers are like silence that has thawed and glistens in the sunlight.

Beside the forest the lake: like a seal stamped by silence on the face of the earth. Or it may suddenly seem like a grey-blue plate fastened on the earth to prevent the silence from breaking through completely and covering up everything.

There are two ships sailing at both ends of the lake, slowly, watchfully, observantly.

A mighty tree stands near the lake. Its heavy

trunk is pressed in the earth like a great stake planted against the silence. But the silence has crept up along the trunk and the crown of the tree spreads itself out to make room for the silence.

The things of nature are filled with silence. They are like great reserves of silence.

The forest is like a great reservoir of silence out of which the silence trickles in a thin, slow stream and fills the air with its brightness.

The mountain, the lake, the fields, the sky— they all seem to be waiting for a sign to empty their silence on to the things of noise in the cities of men.

A bird flies from one side of the valley to the other. And it is as though silence were being thrown through space through the body of the bird as through a ball. The bird's voice is like the sound of the ball cutting through the air, and the silence is even more audible after every note of the bird has sounded.

In the expectant stillness, the silence in things increases. Things seem to sink in the silence, to be merely the outer edge of silence. That is what has happened to the old villages on the hillsides in the Ticino. They have sunk in the silence, like ships resting on the ocean bed of silence, and the clouds above are like brightly coloured fish that, having once upon a time collided with the huge shipwrecks at the bottom of the sea, now keep well away.

The people who walk slowly through these villages are like divers, hauling up the lost treasures of silence from the ocean bed.

Some who have been talking as they have entered these villages have left them full of silence.

3

At the beginning of spring things return from the silence and come back more to themselves.

In the spring when the leaves sit shyly on the branches like butterflies, and the blue sky moves among the branches so that the leaves quiver more in the blue than on the branches, the tree belongs more to the sky and to itself than to the silence.

A deer jumps between two trees, and the bright patch on its coat is like a sound travelling through the silence.

Then all at once the moon appears, and the crescent of the moon is like the opening slit through which the silence trickles down in to the forest and covers everything.

In the heat of the summer noon the silence breaks right into space. Time itself seems to stand still, paralyzed by this sudden jolt.

The vault of the sky is stretched up high, and the sky is like the upper edge of silence.

The earth has sunk down low. Only its edge is visible, the lower edge of silence.

The mountain, the trees, and the scattered houses are like the last things remaining after everything else has been utterly absorbed by the noonday silence. The silence seems calm, as it were coagulated; and it is as though even these last remaining things would vanish as soon as the silence moves.

A bird flies slowly into the sky, and its movements are like dark trails that keep the silence enclosed within itself. It is as though, otherwise, the silence might open in the next moment and draw everything into itself.

Not the darkness but the light belongs to silence. That is never so clear as in the summer noon when the silence is utterly transformed into light.

The silence is as it were uncovered, and light appears as the inwardness of silence.

In these summer noons the silence is quite uncovered, and the light within lies naked to the eye. Nothing moves, nothing dares to move.

The light seems so much the essence of silence that the word seems quite unnecessary. The light is all at once the fulfilment of the silence.

It might well be that the inner light might sometime come out from us so that we should need no other light. (Goethe)

In the night silence moves nearer to the earth. The earth is filled with a silence which seems even to penetrate the very surface of the soil. The words of the daytime are dissolved in the silence of the night.

A bird suddenly begins to sing in the night. And the song is like the residue of the sounds left over by the daytime, which, taking fright, embrace each other in the birdsong and make the song a hiding place.

A boat travels over the lake and the beat of the oars is like a knocking on the wall of silence.

The trees stretch up high into the night as if they were taking something up with them along their trunks and were going to hand it over to the silence. The next morning the trunks are even straighter than the evening before.

Strangers to themselves and suddenly strangers to the place where they are, things stand in the night as though they had not been here in the daytime but had been set down in the night by silence without noticing it themselves. They seem to have travelled in on the silence as on a ship, secretly: as Odysseus was brought to Ithaca and put down on the shore and treasures laid beside him, so things are brought along silently in the night.

4

Sometimes it is as though the silence of nature were in rebellion; as though it wanted to invade the word of man.

The wind rumbles, rushing headlong as it rumbles, as if it were looking for the word and wanted to take the word away from the mouth of man as he speaks: the word vanishes in the rumbling of the wind.

Nature is afraid, when the wind rumbles, lest the silence may leave her and something else take its place.

The silence is gathered together tightly in the storm, but it darts up in the lightning, flashing without thunder through the forest.

There is a fear in the bending of the trees. It is the fear of the creature faced with change and transformation.

But suddenly all is still. Every sound has been shattered in the raging of the wind.

The sea roars. And it is as though it wanted to tear itself open; as if with the soaring waves it wanted to uncover itself.

But suddenly it sinks into itself again as if in the depths it had found the object of its search; and the depth is suddenly covered by its own calm again.

At night the threads of the moon reach down into the depths of the sea like nets. And now when through the silence that lies upon it the sea sinks down into itself, it is as if with the sound of the sea all human sounds have sunk into the sea and man cries out to himself in fear.

Fire . . . When the flame stops a moment in the crackling fire and returns with sudden violence to the ground, then it is as though the fire wanted to fetch something, and so the flame stops for a moment, but then rises higher and more vehemently still and with an ever more intense despair.

5

When the silence in nature is so dense that the things in nature seem to be only more intense condensations of the silence, then it seems as though man, too, ceases to possess the word, and the word is only a chink in the silence.

Is there another country in the world in which the silence is so perfect? Here in the land of the Eskimos there is no wind in the trees, for there are no leaves. No birds sing. There is no noise of flowing water. No frightened animals flee away in the dark. There is no stone to become loose under human feet and fall down a river bank, for all these stones are walled in by the frost and buried under the snow. And yet this word is far from dead: it is only that the beings which dwell in this solitude are noiseless and invisible.

This stillness which had been so solitary, which had calmed me and done good to my worn-out nerves, gradually began to weigh on me like a lead weight. The flame of life within us withdrew further and further into a secret hiding place, and our heart beats became ever slower. The day

would come when we should have to shake ourselves to keep our heart beats going. We had sunk
deep into this silence, we were paralysed by it, we
were on the bottom of a well from which we
could pull ourselves out only with inconceivable
difficulty. (Gontran de Poncins, *Kabluna*)

One can hear man trembling with fear in this
passage lest he be dissolved in the silence and
become merely a part of the silence of nature.
The words seem to have grown in the fear,
thrown like great shadows on the wall of silence,
the silence that comes ever nearer. The words
are like the last attempt to keep back the wall of
silence lest it move any nearer.

The silence of nature presses into man. The
spirit of man is like the sky over the broad surface of this silence. The spirit makes the silence
of nature a part of the human world. It redeems
the silence that is only nature and links it with
that silence from which the word came and in
which there is a mark of the silence of God.

POETRY AND SILENCE

1

Poetry comes out of silence and yearns for silence. Like man himself, it travels from one silence to another. It is like a flight, like a circling over silence.

Just as the floor of a house is inlaid with a mosaic, so the floor of silence is inlaid with poetry. Great poetry is a mosaic inlaid into silence.

This does not mean that in poetry silence is more important than language:

> The highest and the most excellent is not what is inexpressible, as if the poet in himself were of greater depth than his work reveals, but his *works* represent what is best in the artist. . . . But the poet is not what merely remains unexpressed within him. (Hegel)

The great poet does not completely fill out the space of his theme with his words. He leaves a space clear, into which another and higher poet can speak. He allows another to take part in the subject; he makes the subject his own but does not keep it entirely for himself. Such poetry is therefore not rigid and fixed but has a hovering

quality ready at any moment to belong to another, to a still higher poet.

Consider, for instance, an image Goethe uses
to describe something. It does not weigh down
the object it describes; on the contrary, it makes
it light and even transparent.

It is quite different in the work of Ernst
Juenger. He occupies the whole space of the
object with his image; he imprisons it, makes it
defenseless, and not only covers the object but
crushes it to death. He invades and conquers it,
and there is no freedom in such work.

Only where poetry is related with silence is
a monologue feasible: for the individual speaking
is not alone, but stands confronting the silence,
and the monologue is in fact a dialogue with
the silence.

> It would betray great ignorance to disparage the
> monologue and even to call it unnatural. . . . On
> the stage when a great and moving action is passing
> across it, that which unlocks all hearts seems to be
> the least unnatural. (Jacob Grimm)

The space of silence in every true poem must
not be confused with the empty spaces that are
also to be found in all great poetry. This emptiness is no real emptiness, but is like the poverty
that is sometimes found in nature. It is not a
weakness or deficiency. So it is with Gotthelf,
for example: the empty places are like nature

in repose, and therefore they are in fact like
places of authentic silence.

The poet's word not only has a natural relation with the silence from which it comes, but
it can also produce silence through the spirit that
is in it. Through the creative act of the word
the silence that is purely natural is re-created
once again by the spirit. The word can be so
powerful, so absolutely perfect a word, that its
contrary, silence, is automatically present. It is
absorbed by the word: the perfect silence is
heard as the echo of the perfect word.

In the "Prologue in Heaven" in Goethe's *Faust*
a powerful silence is produced by the powerful
word after each verse. There is an active, audible
silence after every verse. The things that were
moved into position by the word stand motionless in the silence, as if they were waiting to be
called back into the silence and to disappear
therein. The word not only brings the things out
of the silence; it also produces the silence in
which they can disappear again. The earth is not
burdened by the things: the word brings them
to the silence in which they float away.

2

Poetry today has lost its relationship with
silence. It comes from the word, from all words,

and mostly there is not even anything to be conveyed by the word. The word is rather searching and hunting for something to convey. But the real poet starts in possession of the object, and goes in search of the words, not *vice versa*.

Today the poet's word goes to all words. It can combine with many things, attract many things to itself; seem more than it really is. In fact the word seems to be as it were sent out to catch other words. And so it comes about that the writer today presents far more than he actually possesses himself. His person is less than what he writes; he is not identical with his work. And he therefore tends to undergo frequent crises on account of this discrepancy. It could happen in earlier times that the poet was different from his work, but his *person* was not so dependent on it, since the work belonged more to the cosmic order of the universe than to the person of the poet. The important thing was not the nature of the subject who had spoken the word but the objective validity of the word. There was no question of a confrontation, and therefore no question of a conflict between the person of the poet and the written word.

We have said that poetry has lost its relationship to silence. It is even demanded of poetry today that it should represent the world of noise; that noise should be audible in poetry as it is everywhere else. It is imagined that that would be the justification of noise, and also that the noise could be overcome by forcing it into rhymed verse. But it is not possible to overcome the noise of the external world with the noise of poetry, for the noise of poetry starts competing with the noise of the external world, and the two noises rattle along beside each other.

Noise can be overcome only by something that is utterly different. Orpheus did not overcome the underworld by becoming as dark as the underworld but by the wholly different bright sound of his song.

3

A word that participates in the world of silence expresses something quite different from the same word that is far removed from silence. That is why it is difficult to interpret Hölderlin, for example, with the words of today. But precisely because we feel that the words of today no longer correspond to the same words of an earlier age, we are always trying to understand the old words. We are shut out from the language of Hölderlin and yet outwardly we are still near to it; and this fact stimulates us to make attempt after attempt to penetrate it. The words of such poets, which live on their connection with silence, are almost unintelligible today. They are mysterious hieroglyphs, the hieroglyphs of silence.

Hölderlin seems to stand silently today in a

row with Laotse, Sophocles, Shakespeare, Goethe, all of whom are also silent; and standing beside each other thus, their nature becomes visible in the silence. Their true form becomes so visible that the original word could arise again out of the fullness of this concretely visible nature.

EXAMPLES

PRIMITIVE RACES

"But where did my soul go?
Come home, come home.
It travelled far South,
South of the peoples to the South of us.
Come home, come home.

But where did my soul go?
Come home, come home.
It travelled far East,
East of the peoples to the East of us.
Come home, come home.

But where did my soul go?
Come home, come home.
It travelled far North,
North of the peoples to the North of us.
Come home, come home.

But where did my soul go?
Come home, come home.
It travelled far West,
West of the peoples to the West of us.
Come home, come home."
                          (Eskimo song after Rasmussen)

In this song it seems as though language hardly dares to exist. It is already separated from silence but not yet sure of itself. It repeats itself continuously as if it wanted to learn how to live, and were afraid of disappearing. It is as though the song continues to sound even when the singer is asleep. The sounds are engraven in the air as in a gramophone record of silence. There is great melancholy in the songs of primitive races, the melancholy of the man who has a double fear: he is afraid because he is being expelled from silence by the word, and he is afraid of being thrown back again into the silence and losing the word again. The melancholy of the song moves on endlessly between these two fears, which are as endless as silence and endless as language.

Primitive man is greatly afraid of losing language, and that is why he repeats it so often. The word of the song is a watchman in the night which covers the silence. As the fire scares away hostile animals, so the words of the song scare away the hostile silence that is waiting to devour them.

THE FAIRY STORY

The events in fairy stories are quite simple.

The parents have no more bread and have to turn out their children in this extremity, or a hard stepmother lets them suffer and would even like to leave them to die. Then brother and sister are forsaken in the solitude of the wood; they are frightened by the winter, but they stand by each other

through thick and thin; the little brother knows
how to find the way home again or the little sister
is changed by magic into a little fawn and looks
for plants and moss to make her brother a bed; or
she sits quietly sewing a shirt with star-shaped
flowers which destroys the magic spell. The whole
circle of this fairy-tale world is definite and closed;
kings, princes, faithful servants and honest crafts-
men, above all, fishermen, millers, charcoal-burners
and shepherds, who have remained close to nature,
appear therein; everything outside this closed
circle is foreign to it. (Jacob Grimm)

The words and actions in fairy stories are so
simple that they can disappear quite easily at any
moment. They do not have to disengage first
from a complicated world. The poverty of the
fairy story comes from the fact that nothing in
it is fixed: everything is ready to give itself up
and disappear again.

Meanwhile, however, the great stars speak
with little children, horses with kings, and even
trees have the power of language and call out
to men. In the fairy story it is not yet quite
certain whether the stars or the flowers and the
trees or man will receive the power of language:
everything is still subject to revocation, everything is merely provisional. It is as though the
silence in the depths of the story were considering to whom it should give language forever—
to the stars, the trees, or to man. Man received
the word, but for a time the trees and stars and
animals continued to speak, too.

In the genuine fairy tale everything must be strange, mysterious, and incoherent. . . . The whole of nature must be mixed up with the spirit world in a wonderful way; it is the age of universal anarchy, the freedom and natural state of nature before the foundation of the world. This age before the creation of the world, just as the state of primitive nature, is a strange image of the eternal kingdom. (Novalis)

Every event in a fairy story is like a new beginning, the example of a new law that might form the basis of a world different from our own. There is an abundance of possible worlds in the fairy story, and therefore an infinite wealth streams out from it. The mystery is that the human world, the world in which only man has speech, is the only possibility that has been realized. The fairy story leads us to revere this mystery. The world of silence becomes brighter and more radiant whilst the colourful world of fairy tales lies over it.

Everything in the fairy tale has really happened before it happens. The words follow after the things rather than precede and announce them. Everything is already at hand before the words begin to tell the story. Everything could happen silently, without words at all. The fact that what could happen silently is accompanied by words is a fairy story in itself.

Fairy tales belong to the world of silence, just as children belong to it. And therefore children and fairy tales belong to each other.

PROVERBS

Consider for example: "The pitcher goes so often to the well that it comes home broken at last". Once upon a time a sentence like that seemed to have just emerged from the silence. It presented a concrete picture of the pitcher, the way to the well, and the well itself. One saw the pitcher being turned on the potter's wheel; one heard the water fall from the well into the pitcher, and people walking backward and forward from their home to the well. The sentence was so stable and secure that it seemed quite independent of man. It seemed to exist even before it was ever spoken by man; it seemed to have existed before the creation of man, to be more *for* man than spoken by man.

But in the modern world, which has lost the relationship to silence and all coherence within itself, the pitcher, the well, and the way to the well have been torn apart. The pitcher really is broken. Such a proverb has to be as it were glued together from the broken fragments, like a broken memory of an unbroken world, excavated from its ruins, glued together into a sentence that no one really understands any longer.

Once proverbs were like the beginning of a world, tablets inscribed at the beginning of the world. But today they are the end of a world, the last remaining sentences, the last words gathered together into integrated sentences in a disintegrating world.

CLASSICAL TRAGEDY

It is as though the things and the events had existed long before the words, and as though it had needed time for the words to arrive and give names to them. This silent time is in the drama of antiquity. It is sometimes as if the things were going their own way silently and menacingly, still belonging wholly to the world of silence, followed by the words, which want to hold them fast.

This heroic world of the drama of classical antiquity, this "useless world, containing nothing but conflicts, royal tragedies and gods", as Jakob Burckhardt describes it, this world needs the background of silence, which is itself "the greatest of all useless existences".

The chief actors in the drama of classical antiquity were the gods, and man played only a subsidiary rôle. The gods accompanied men and things; their silence was present in men and things. "We learn silence from the gods, speech from man" (Plutarch). In classical tragedy the silence of the gods is heard in the speaking of man. Man speaks in order to hear this silence; he dies to hear it. When the hero dies, it is as though the silence of the gods were alive and speaking alone.

The chorus is in the centre between the word of man and the silence of the gods. Through the chorus the word of man is surrendered to the silence of the gods. It stops here, in the chorus, before passing into the silence of the gods, and it stops here, too, when it comes from the silence of the gods.

The heroes of antiquity spoke to men, but there was more silence than speech in their actions, and they were silent as before the gods. The words they spoke merely followed the lines of the silence already traced out by the gods. And because the words were always vanishing over the lines of the silence, they were repeated again and again. "Thy fame will shine on thee in the whole world and for ever, Achilles."

THE PRE-SOCRATICS

Every sentence seems to have arisen directly from the silence. The sentences still seem amazed to find they exist at all. The words are still rubbing the sleep from their eyes; they are still not fully themselves; they are still half way between sleep and waking. They speak in order to make certain of themselves, to hear themselves. They can hardly believe that they are in the world of waking and the world of words.

Man lights a light for himself in the night, because he is dead and yet still alive. In sleep he touches himself as dead when the light of his eyes has faded but in waking he touches himself not dead but only asleep. (Heraclitus)

Nothing in this sentence is there for its own sake: one thing merges into another. Sleep is not yet a strictly defined sleep, but it touches death and it touches life. Everything is still a little helpless. Everything is still holding everything else by the hand. Waking holds sleep by the hand and sleep reaches out for death. Neither wants to be left entirely on its own.

Words have not yet found a real home in the world of words; they have not yet found any real home at all. They are words fallen out of the dream of silence and pressing on into the silence of the gods. But a part of them sank down like meteor stones into the world of man, confusing human words with their silence, with the silence that belongs to the gods.

HERODOTUS

The objects, the events, exist concretely, and their concrete existence is a story in itself. It is as though the objects and the events were telling each other rather than man about themselves— the objects and events are so concretely primary, and the man reporting them so secondary. That is possible only when the word betakes itself to the object and the event as it were for the first time, to the object and event to which it belongs, and to which it therefore holds fast so that word and object are a unity.

In later ages, too, in which words and objects are constantly being manipulated, it is still possible for the poet to restore the unity of word and object in such a way as to make it seem as if word and object were meeting for the first time and forever; as if the objects were telling what they are through their pure existence, without the mediation of language.

It is thus in the *Schatzkästlein* of Johann Peter Hebel. It is as though the objects in these stories had escaped from a noisy, disrupted and disrupting world into a secluded valley and were there telling each other about themselves, as if there were no men listening; passing the time with memories and jokes and waiting here in the secluded valley for the world to return in which that happens in every moment which happened once to them: that the word holds them fast against false and unnecessary mobility, against being manipulated.

There are no longer any silent men in the world today; there is no longer even any difference between the silent and the speaking man, only between the speaking and the non-speaking man. And because there are no silent men there are also no longer any listeners. Man today is incapable of listening; and because he is incapable of listening he can no longer tell a story, for listening and true story-telling belong together: they are a unity.

In the stories of the *Schatzkästlein* one hears not only the story-teller but also the silence of those who listen. And one hears how, after this silence, the listener himself begins to tell a story, for listening and story-telling take turns.

SHAKESPEARE

The words and the scenes are as new and alive as if they had just jumped this very moment from silence into language. The element of language is still new to them. They frisk about in it like young animals let out of an enclosure for the first time. They run along in long rows. Some face each other like hostile armies. Some climb over each other exuberantly. But there are words lonely as sentries waiting for something (Ophelia's words in *Hamlet*, for example.) The most beautiful words are formed into images, images that are like heraldic figures, like signs proclaiming that the word not only exists here but resides in ceremonious splendour.

JEAN PAUL

Everything in Jean Paul is there at once: it does not develop, it reveals itself. It is a poetry that moves from word to word but is static as a totality, hovering over silence like a gentle cloud; and the verbal images are like visions of silence. The magic of this language consists in the synthesis of motion from word to word and the motionlessness of the whole structure: movement and stillness are one.

The words are like the wings of a great bird rising above the surface of silence and casting a broad shadow as it flies.

HÖLDERLIN

The words come as it were out of a space that existed before the beginning of creation. This space behind creation echoes solemnly and almost menacingly in the words. The unknown, the terrifying, and also the forsaken in Hölderlin's poetry come from that. The word calls to man through the antechamber of creation. It is like the word that speaks before man has been created: vibrant with yearning for man.

GOETHE

NIGHT SONG

Oh, gib vom weichen Pfuehle,
Traeumend ein halb Gehoer!
Bei meinem Saitenspiele
Schlafe! Was willst du mehr?

Bei meinem Saitenspiele
Segnet der Sterne Heer

Die ewigen Gefuehle;
Schlafe! Was willst du mehr?

Die ewigen Geguehle
Heben mich, hoch und hehr,
Aus irdischem Gewuehle;
Schlafe! was willst du mehr?

Vom irdischen Gewuehle
Trennst du mich nur zu sehr,
Bannst mich in diese Kuehle;
Schlafe! was willst du mehr?

Bannst mich in diese Kuehle,
Gibst nur im Traum Gehoer.
Ach, auf dem weichen Pfuehle
Schlafe! was willst du mehr?

Just as children shout outside the house of a
playmate they are waiting for, so the words of
the lover cry out here for a word from the beloved; not noisily like the children, but quietly,
for the words of the beloved are enclosed in
sleep. It is as though the lover were trying to
entice the words of the beloved out of dreams.
Like gentle, velvet balls the words glide over
the sleeping beloved. Like the dew of silence
it falls back on the word from the beloved.

THE PLASTIC ARTS
AND SILENCE

THE COLONNADES of the Greek temples are like boundary lines along the silence. They become ever straighter and ever whiter as they lean against the silence.

It is as though the colonnade could continue, column by column, into infinity. Thus the gods create, silently, inaudibly. These columns seem to have come from the workshop of the gods.

Wandering amongst the Egyptian pillars is like wandering into the dark, into what lies behind. Although one is really walking on the level earth, one seems to be walking down the steps into a cavern, finally reaching the place of death. It is the way to an ever increasing silence. The words of the Egyptians echoed from this subterranean cavern of death.

Wandering amongst the Greek pillars is a wandering in a radiant silence. Silence and radiance are one. It is a silence that signifies the moment of rest before the new creation—silence and creation alternated. It was like a staircase

to Olympus, where, with the gods, silence and
creation became one and alternated no more.

The ruined pillars, and the ruined temples . . .
It is as though before the invasion of noise, silence
burst open, and in bursting, tore the temple to
pieces. The blocks of marble and the columns
try in vain to sink back with the silence into the
earth. They have been thrown back again and
smashed again by the foundered silence.

The stillness that now reigns round the temples
is not the stillness of silence, but the stillness of
the grave. Silence here has its grave, and the
white columns and blocks of marble are the
tombstones over the sunken silence.

THE GREEK STATUES, THE EGYPTIAN STATUES

The Greek statues were like vessels of silence.
They stood there in rows, and man passed between them as along an avenue of silence.

The silence was confined in the statues and
became a splendour over their whiteness.

Their silence is full of mystery. It is as though
they remain silent as long as man stands before
them and as if they begin to speak as soon as they
are alone. They speak to the gods, but they are
silent to man.

The marble statues of the Greek gods lie
embedded like white islands of silence in the
midst of the noise of the world today. The old
white statues of the gods are the remains the

silence left behind when it had to retire from the noise of today.

The silence that is in the Greek statues does not oppress them: it is a light and radiant silence. The figure is master over the silence: at any moment the word can arise from the silence like a god from Olympus.

The Egyptian statues, on the other hand, are absolutely subjugated by the silence: they are prisoners of the silence. The eye belongs to the gods, the mouth belongs to the gods so that it may express their silence.

It was not the stone that made the figures heavy and prevented them from moving; it was the silence which surrounded them and which they dared not touch.

In the faces of the old Egyptians, in these rigid faces, there is still the fear that was in the world before the word attained supremacy over silence. It is like a relapse into the time in which there was still no word, and that is the reason the Egyptian faces move man today more than those of the Greeks: in the modern world of violent noise man is homesick for the world beyond all sound and beyond all language.

Here in the Egyptian face of the oldest periods the silence is not amicably disposed to language as it is in the Greek face; it is a silence imperiously hostile to language.

The sculptures of the Egyptians show a more lifeless seriousness, an undisclosed mystery, so that the figure represented suggests not its own individual inner life but a more remote significance of which it is still unaware itself. (Hegel)

Some Egyptian faces look as though they had seen silence naked and as though the sight had paralysed them. As in early times an animal was enclosed by the solidifying resin of trees, by amber, so the Egyptian face is enclosed by silence.

The Egyptian figures are turned inwards. It is as though there were a second figure inside the more important one, to which the first is speaking—or rather speaking in the silence, without words.

The Greek face, on the other hand, is turned outward. There is no fear in it of that world in which the word has not yet appeared; it directs itself towards a world out of which the word comes. There is a certainty expressed in it, that in every moment the silence can be overcome by the word, matter by spirit; and therefore there is often a serenity and always a freedom in it. The silence does not go back to something past, to a world without language, but to a present and a future, to the world of language. And precisely for that reason the Greek face goes through all ages and is even present with us today.

THE EGYPTIAN PYRAMIDS

They are oppressive, because it is as if they had the power to extend much further out over the earth and towards the sky than they do.

Only because they are related to the order of the stars which is recorded in them they do not press on further.

They are oppressive because it is as though the masses of stone were not kept back by man, nor by any human order, but by the extra-human, by the stars.

The silence of the stars looks down upon them and casts a spell on them.

Not only the dead are buried in the pyramids, not only the silence of the dead, but also the silence of the stars.

The pyramids seem like fortifications, built by silence for itself when it retired from the earth; from which silence can conquer the earth again one day.

THE EGYPTIAN SPHINX

The Egyptian sphinx is not silence but the abyss of silence.

The lines of its body are like the lines of an incantation over the abyss. They are like signs that cast a spell over the abyss.

As after a violent battle the spirits of the

fallen go on fighting in the air; as the image of
the battle stays in the air, so the sphinx remains
from the time of the most violent silence, as an
image of that silence, still with us today. After
all silence has disappeared, it is still with us,
always threateningly ready to invade the world
of noise.

THE ARCHAIC FIGURES

The archaic colossi, the stone memorials in
Sardinia, the stone masses in the palaces at
Mycene . . . Everything that is not silence is
compressed by the stone.

These colossi of silence are so mighty that it
is as though they could take language and everything in language from man and make it disappear within them.

In the silence of these stones everything is
distinct. Words no longer lie over things: they
have been as it were absorbed by them and
have vanished in the silence of the stone.

Ekbatana, the city of the Medes, had seven
circular walls, each with different coloured bat-
tlements. They were, according to Herodotus,
the heavenly spheres enclosing the sun castle, and
the obelisks were sunrays in stone. No word
could express so well the power of the heavenly
spheres as this monument in the silence of stone.
In the silence of these stones the heavenly spheres

and the rays of the sun lived again on earth, and in their silence one heard their movement in the sky.

Every word spoken before this archaic stone was an invasion of the silence that belongs to the gods. The silence was present so intensely that it seemed as if the word itself might be petrified at any moment into a colossus, just as the rays of the sun had become petrified into an obelisk and the orbit of the stars into stone circles.

But the archaic figures —they are excavated more from the silence than from the earth. They are like the ruins of silence. If the eye travels along them it is as though it were travelling along the silence. The face is furrowed with silence: the lines, the surfaces, are spread out on the silence, are carried by it. And the whole figure is penetrated by the silence.

The human form seems to be preserved here forever in the silence. Not a single line of the face dares to move in the silence.

THE CHINESE GATES

The Chinese gates, which rise in solitude from the surface of the Chinese plain, joined to no wall or building . . . Infinite is the plain, infinite is the silence. Nothing moves through the gate but the silence. The roundness of the gate is like a cavern dug out by silence for itself. Sacred images of the gods and sacred animals are by the gate like sentries and retinue at the same time.

Sometimes it is as though many invisible arches were moving over the one visible arch, moving upwards, each vaulted over the other, moving like a ladder upwards into heaven. The silence itself climbs up to heaven on this vaulting ladder.

CHINESE PAINTING

Chinese pictures are like figures in a moonlit mist over the world of silence, woven from moon threads over the silence.

It is as if the object had fallen into silence, as if silence had crystallized around them. A leaf falls into the silence, and the silence settles round the leaf and enfolds it. It is completely enclosed by the silence; it becomes transparent in the silence; it has become the centre, the focus of the silence.

In such a picture live on the thousands of years that silence needed until it could enfold the leaf within itself. There is time and continuity in it. Time itself has come to its end, when the silence has finally enwrapped the leaf wholly within itself.

THE CATHEDRALS

Silence has locked itself up in cathedrals and protected itself with walls.

Just as ivy grows round a wall for centuries, so the cathedrals have grown round the silence. They are built around the silence.

The silence of a Romanesque cathedral exists as a substance, so that it is as though the cathedral, by the very fact of its existence, were producing walls of silence, cities of silence, men of silence; giving birth to them as if it were a huge pregnant animal.

The cathedrals are like silence inlaid with stone.

Figures stand at the corners of the pillars: messengers, who were intended to carry the silence into the city of man. Just as one sends out servants with vessels to bring water, so they were supposed to bring the silence—but in the silence they forgot to move on.

The cathedrals stand like enormous reservoirs of silence. There is no word inside them: the word becomes music and song over the depths of an even greater silence.

The cathedral tower is like a heavy ladder on which the silence climbs into heaven, to fade and disappear therein. In an arch it falls down again, to the tower of another cathedral. In this arch of silence all cathedrals are connected with one another.

The cathedrals are deserted today, just as silence is deserted. They have become museums of silence, but they are still inter-related, cathedral with cathedral, silence with silence. They stand like ichthyosauri of silence, no longer understood by any one. It was inevitable that they should be bombarded in the war: absolute noise shooting at absolute silence.

Sometimes a cathedral looks like a great ark into which all men and animals are being gathered to be saved from the flood of noise. A bird sits on the edge of the roof, and the notes of its song are like a knocking on the wall of silence, asking it to come in.

THE PICTURES OF THE OLD MASTERS

The figures have let their words fall down into the silence. The gold background is the silence, which has trickled through the words of the sacred figures.

The pictures of the old masters are filled to bursting point with silence: so full of silence that one expects the word to emerge at any moment —but what comes is only a greater silence.

The figures are a radiance over the world of

silence. They allow the silence to make and keep
them silent and therefore they are radiant. In the
radiance they are trying to hear the silence; they
stand motionless in the radiance and hearken to
the silence.

PIERO DELLA FRANCESCA

In his pictures not only the objects are there,
but with them the ideas of the objects as well,
as certainly as the objects themselves: the Platonic world of ideas is visible in these pictures.
Everything is ready for departure into a new
reality where idea and appearance are one; as if
in the last moment before this journey idea and
object are together. The eye of the gods falls on
these figures as on to the Platonic ideas in a space
above the world, and they increase in size and
substance in the silence of the eye gazing down
on them.

Piero della Francesca's human beings seem to
wander in a dream of the gods, before the gods
created man. Through this wandering in the
dream of the gods they are full of silence.

Sometimes they are also like the dreams that
silence dreams itself, before it sends things out
into the room of wide-awake reality.

The figures have sunk down into silence, like
cities lost beneath the ocean. They are preserved
under the water of silence just as prehistoric

animals are preserved under the soil of the earth.

Just as water drips down from the face of one coming out of the sea, silence drips down these faces. The human beings in the pictures of Piero della Francesca possess silence like a new sense; they speak through silence as if it were a new language. Sometimes they seem like shadows, bright shadows thrown by the world of silence into the world of noise. They become bigger and bigger as if they were straining to grow into the world of noise, to grow beyond it and covering it, inaudibly to take command over it.

THE NOISE OF WORDS

TODAY WORDS no longer rise out of silence, through a creative act of the spirit which gives meaning to language and to the silence, but from other words, from the noise of other words. Neither do they return to the silence but into the noise of other words, to become immersed therein.

Language has lost its spiritual quality; all that remains is its purely acoustic quality. This is the transformation of the spirit into the material, the transformation of the word that is spirit into the material of noise.

The noise of words is the loud emptiness that covers the soundless emptiness. The real word, on the other hand, is the loud fullness over the still surface of silence.

There is a difference between ordinary noise and the noise of words. Noise is the enemy of silence; it is opposed to silence. The noise of words is not merely opposed to silence: it makes us even forget that there was ever any such thing as silence at all. It is not even an acoustical phenomenon: the acoustic element, the continual buzzing of verbal noise, is merely a sign that all space and all time have been filled by it.

Ordinary noise, on the other hand, is limited, closely related to a definite object, a notification of that object. The noise of a festive gathering or of peasant music is edged around with a silence which gives intensity and prominence to the noise. The silence is as it were stationed on the frontiers of the noise, waiting for the time when it can appear again. But only emptiness and nothingness are stationed in the frontiers of verbal noise.

Words no longer arise from silence today but from other words, from the noise of other words. The word that arises from silence, on the other hand, moves from the silence into the word and then back again into the silence, out of the silence to the new word and back again into the silence and so on, so that the word always comes from the centre of silence. The flow of the sentence is continually broken by a silence. The vertical barriers of silence are constantly interrupting the horizontal flow of the sentence.

Mere verbal noise, on the other hand, moves uninterruptedly along the horizontal line of the sentence. The only important thing seems to be that the noise should go on without interruption, not that it should mean anything.

Cityful passing away, other cityful coming, passing away too: other coming on, passing on. Houses, lines of houses, streets, miles of pavements, piled up bricks, stones. Changing hands. This owner, that. Landlord never dies they say. Other steps into his shoes when he gets notice to quit. They buy the place up with gold and still they have all the gold. Swindle in it somewhere. Piled up in cities, worn away age after age. Pyramids in sand. Built on bread and onions. Slaves. Chinese wall. Babylon. Big stones left. Round towers. Rest rubble, sprawling suburbs, jerrybuilt, Kerwan's mushroom houses, built of breeze. Shelter for the night.

No one is anything.

This is the very worst hour of the day. Vitality. Dull, gloomy: hate this hour. Feel as if I had been eaten and spewed.

James Joyce.

That is an example of the language of verbal noise.

In this so-called language subject, predicate, object, and adverbs are all mixed up together. The sentence becomes an almost amorphous mass of sound, out of which a single sound occasionally booms forth more prominently than the others. Such words are mere intimations, mere notifications of something: they do not go so far as to mean anything. (One can say that meanings are conveyed even by verbal noise. That is quite right. But the meaning conveyed is a merely material statement of fact; a true meaning is possible only when the word refers, draws attention to the infinity of the thing described [Husserl]. This quality of infinity, which can never be completely expressed or exhausted by words, is present in silence. In verbal noise, therefore, it is true that material meanings are conveyed, but the medium in which the meaning appears—the medium of verbal noise —is hostile to the very nature of meaning; it outweighs and swallows up the meaning.)

Language has become a mere mechanical vehicle transporting the outward signs of language.

Language has ceased to be organic and plastic, ceased to establish things firmly. Words have become merely signs that something is being fetched out of the jumble of noise and thrown at the listener. The word is not specifically a word. It can now be replaced by signs—colour signs or sound signs; it has become an apparatus, and like every mere apparatus it is always facing the possibility of destruction. And therefore the man who does not live directly from the word, but allows himself to be dragged along by the apparatus of noise, also faces destruction at any moment.

These verbal noises do not seem to be spoken by men at all: they are verbal ghosts coming from the world of dead words, talking amongst themselves, one dead word with another, and happy if two or three have happened to form themselves into a consecutive sentence, just as ghosts are happy when they meet each other in a ghostly place.

> The destruction of life consists in turning it into an enemy. Life is immortal and when killed it seems like the awful ghost of itself. (Hegel)

The destruction of the word consists in turning it into the enemy, but not an enemy that confronts but one that penetrates and permeates us like a ghost.

Contrast a sentence from the world of real words, a sentence from J. P. Hebel:

> It is curious that a man who seems to be without much substance can impart wisdom to another who regards himself as exceptionally wise and understanding.

In this sentence each part is exact in itself, conscious of its value, standing on its own, yet all the words are related to something higher. "It is curious": these words create the space for an event. It is as though they were drawing a cord round a room so that something definite can happen therein. And with the last word "curious" it is as if one could see a board announcing that something remarkable was about to take place here. "That sometimes a man": a man appears in this marked-off space, hesitantly: "sometimes" is the sign that he is hesitating. "Who seems to be without much substance": the man seems small in this big space. One waits to see what is going to happen to him, and it happens: "that he can impart wisdom to another". And all at once the hesitant little man seems big and the man who "regards himself as exceptionally wise and understanding" becomes small. It is as though the "exceptional wisdom and understanding" were taken from him like so much baggage that does not belong to him.

Every word in this sentence of Hebel shows that the sentence is firmly established. This word is so secure and the words in it so secure, that the world needs only a little sentence like that to make known that it exists. A whole world and all the words of this world stand close to this sentence.

2

The verbal noise by which the real word is replaced today does not arise from a definite act, like the word. It is not actively begotten, but produced by proliferation—that is to say: one noise divides to produce another noise. The real word is created in the qualitative, verbal noise in the quantitative, sphere.

Verbal noise seems in fact never to have been specifically created. It seems to have always been there. There does not seem to be any space left where there could possibly ever have been anything but noise. It has infiltrated into everything. We take it for granted much as we take the air itself for granted. Everything begins and ends with noise. It does not seem to depend for its existence on man at all: it seems to be something objective outside him. The noise of words is not spoken by man at all: it is simply spoken all around him. It penetrates him, fills him up to the very brim, and the noise is what overflows through the edge of his mouth.

Nobody listens to him as he speaks, for listening is only possible when there is silence in man: listening and silence belong together. Instead of truly speaking to others today we are all waiting merely to unload on to others the words that have collected inside us. Speech has become a purely animal, excretive function.

Verbal noise is neither silence nor sound. It permeates silence and sound alike and it causes man to forget both silence and the world.

There has ceased to be any difference between speech and silence, since one single noise of words permeates both the speaker and the non-speaker. The silent listener has simply become a non-speaker.

Verbal noise is a peusdo-language and a pseudo-silence. That is to say, something is spoken and yet it is not real language at all. Something disappears in the noise and yet it is not real silence. When the noise suddenly stops, it is not followed by silence, but merely a pause in which the noise accumulates in order to expand with even greater force when it is released.

It is as though the noise were afraid that it might disappear, as if it were constantly on the move, because it must always be convincing itself that it really exists. It does not believe in its own existence.

The real word, on the contrary, has no such

fear, even when it is not being expressed in sound: its existence is in fact even more palpable in the silence.

Man, however, who has become a mere appendage of verbal noise, believes decreasingly in the reality of his own existence. He looks at himself in the thousands of pictures on the screen and in the illustrated papers, as if he were trying to make sure that man still exists, still looks like man.

Man is so unreal today that in a room in front of great mirrors people do not look real but as if they had come out of the reflections in the mirror, sent out for a holiday. And when the lights are switched off they seem to fall back into the mirror and disappear in its darkness.

But where silence is still an active force, man is constantly re-created by the word that comes out of the silence, and constantly disappearing in the silence before God. His existence is a continuous creation in the word through God and a disappearing in the silence before God.

Today his existence is merely a continuous emerging from the noise of words and a continuous disappearing therein.

3

Language is so conditioned by its origin in the *Logos*, which is order, that it does not admit into the human world much that lies outside the human order. Language is a protection for man. Many demonic things are waiting to invade man and to destroy him, but man is protected from contact with the demonic; indeed he is unable even to notice it because it does not enter into language: the word defends man from the invasion of the demonic. But only if man preserved the word in its true nature is it able to maintain its power against evil. The noise of words which is the modern substitute for language is perforated and therefore open to penetration by the powers of the demonic.

Everything can steal into the noise of words; everything can get mixed up in it, even the demonic. In fact the noise is itself a part of the demonic.

In the noise everything is propagated in all directions. Antisemitism, class warfare, national socialism, bolshevism, literature—everything spreads itself out in all directions. Everything has arrived everywhere before man comes on the scene at all. Everything is there waiting for him. All limits and frontiers become blurred, all standards are destroyed. The real word sets up frontiers. The noise of words leaps over the frontiers, ignores them altogether.

In this world of verbal noise a war easily becomes "total" because war can easily take over everything for its own ends. Everything is al-

ready mixed up with war before it seizes hold
of everything.

In this verbal noise everything can be said and
everything abolished and annulled. It is in fact
annulled even before it is said. The most stupid
and the most intelligent things can be said only
to be levelled out, for the main thing is the
general sound of the noise, not what produces
the noise. Whether it is produced by good or by
evil is of no account. This is the mechanism of
irresponsibility at work.

In this world of verbal noise, in which one
thing passes into another, where everything is in
everything else, there are no frontiers outside
and no frontiers inside man. Everyone has access
to everything, everyone understands everything.
And it cannot simply happen that someone (like
Goethe) cannot understand Hölderlin, or someone (like Jakob Burkhardt) deliberately keeps
away from Rembrandt (where there is a real
person, there is a frontier in the person: that is
the very essence and nature of true persons).
But here in the noise of words no one is ex-
cluded from having Goethe and Hölderlin and
Rembrandt and Jakob Burkhardt: everything is
accessible to everyone.

Everything therefore is carried along in the
noise, and any and everything can develop out
of it. Nothing arises any longer through a specific

act, through a decision and through the creative. Everything turns up automatically: through a kind of mimicry the noise produces what is required by the circumstances of the moment, and this is conveyed to man.

For example, if the surrounding world is Nazi, then Nazi ideas are conveyed by the noise, and this takes place *without man's having decided for Nazidom by a special act of his own conscience.* Man is so much a part of the verbal noise going on all around him that he does not notice what is being conveyed to him.

When a new situation appears, then the noise stops conveying Nazi ideas to him—or rather when it has become bored with the prevailing idea it changes its note just for the sake of a change. The attitude of man is dependent on the movement of the noise, no longer on his own will. Man no longer lives with and through the word. The word is no longer the place where man decides for truth or for love: the noise itself makes the decision for him. The noise is the main thing: man is only the place occupied by the noise, the space for the noise to fill.

The noise is also no longer a deposit of the action: it is already part of the action and that is what makes it dangerous.

The real word, on the other hand, comes from the *Logos*. It is maintained by the continuity and the discipline of the *Logos*, and is checked in its movement by its relation with the *Logos*, which takes it into the depths and away from the horizontal rush of mere noise. The action man undertakes does not therefore arise directly from the word but comes from a greater depth, from the place where the word arose from the *Logos*. Therefore the action is not fastened to the word, but at a still deeper level, to the *Logos*. And therefore such an action is protected from the perils of unrestrained license.

In the general verbal noise of today, actions have no foothold, no frontiers, no control, because they are not kept within proper bounds by the word. They are in fact covered by the noise all around them. They disappear therein and real actions have ceased to exist.

This therefore is the world that moves automatically with noise and action. It seems like a world of magic, for everything takes place in it without human decision, of its own accord. And precisely this appearance of magic is what seduces man.

4

In the world of verbal noise, individual events lack a specific character of their own, a character that gives them a special face, just as each individual person has been given a special face.

C'est un des plus grands mystères qu'il y ait dans l'histoire et dans la réalité, et naturellement aussi, naturellement donc l'un donc de ceux sur qui l'on

passe le plus aveuglement, le plus aisément, le plus
inattentivement, le plus sans sauter, que cette espèce
de différence absolue, qu'il y a dans le prix des
événements. Que certains événements soient d'un
certain prix, aient un certain prix, un prix propre.
Que des événements différents du même ordre ou
d'ordre voisins, ayant la même matière ou des
matières du même ordre et de même valeur, aient
pourtant des prix, des valeurs infiniment différ-
entes: que chaque événement opérant une même
matière, faisant devenir une même matière, sous
une même forme, dans une même forme, que tout
événement ait pourtant un prix propre, mystérieux,
une force propre en soi, une valeur propre,
mystérieuse . . . (Péguy)

In the world of verbal noise, events are no
longer distinct from each other: the noise makes
them all the same. That is why events today take
on such big dimensions; that is why they shout
and shriek at us. It is as if one event were trying
to separate itself from all the others by making
as much noise as possible, since it can no longer
do so naturally.

A recent book deals with "The Year 1848 in
Europe", a compilation of the events, day by day,
of the whole year. Many things happened in
1848. Whole nations rose in revolt; kings fell;
the workers were more dissatisfied than ever;
the rich resisted their claims more than ever;
new great powers—Italy and Germany—began
to shape uneasily; wars began or seemed to be
threatening; no day passed without some exciting
news; the whole earth was full of new events—

and one might perhaps think that this superabundance of events was of the same kind as the jumble of events today. But it would be quite wrong to think so.

Every event that occurred in 1848 was clearly distinct from every other event, unmistakably itself, not interchangeable with any other event, having its own physiognomy and its own particular and unique effect. And above all, a special act was necessary in order that it might exist at all, and it did really exist, absolutely, uniquely, and specifically. It was valid in its own right and not merely because of the excitement all around it. The medium in which it existed was first created by the event itself.

It is the other way around today. First comes the medium—namely, the verbal noise; *that* is the important thing. It attracts the event, that is to say, it forms out of itself something into something that looks like an event. But the event is not a specific phenomenon: it is merely a condensation, a concentration of the noise, no more than that. And that is why all events are similar, and also why they arouse so little interest. People do not bother about politics today because they are bored by events. Events are easily forgotten, and man does not even need to forget them himself: the noise does it for him.

If events were not dissolved in the noise, if they were still real, then it would be impossible for them to follow each other so quickly. For a real event needs a certain measure of time; there is a definite relationship between the reality of an event and its duration. A real event needs to acquire its own duration from the duration of time. When an event no longer endures in time, but only emerges for a moment and then disappears again, it becomes a phantom.

Until about 1920 there was still a reality in events and institutions: that is to say, the verbal noise still moved around something, some clearly distinguishable thing. This movement of the noise round a thing was already becoming stereotyped, but it was still possible to recognize the type of literature around which the noise made its din, namely, expressionism, and this expressionism still seemed more important than the noise all around it. It was still possible to distinguish the idea of "social relief"; although the noise of words was churning all around it and covering it, it was even still possible to see political principles more clearly than the noise of words around them.

That is all completely changed today. It is no longer the object that makes the noise around it, as in former times, but the noise is now primary, it *seeks out* an object. It and the object are no longer clearly distinguishable. Routine and object have become immersed in one single noise. It is true that people still talk about this or that particular literary or political object today, but they are only signposts within the noise, merely

the places where the objects are taken up into
the general noise and where man follows after
them, in order to disappear with them in the
noise.

5

The noise of words levels everything down,
makes everything the same: it is a levelling machine. Individuality is a thing of the past. Everyone is merely a part of the noise. Nothing belongs
to the individual any longer. Everything has
been as it were poured into the general noise.
Everyone is entitled to everything because nothing belongs to anyone in particular. The masses
have acquired a status of their own. They are
the complement of the noise and, like the noise,
they are and yet are not, emerging and disappearing, filling everything and yet nowhere
tangible.

The noise of words is so far-ranging, so im-
mense and incalculable, that it is impossible
either to see where it begins and ends or for man
to see where he himself begins and ends. The
noise is like a swarm of insects: all one sees is
a hazy cloud, a cloud of insects giving out a buzz
that covers and equalizes everything.

Man waits for something to come and tear this
vague noise apart by a sharp, piercing sound.
He is tired of the monotone of the buzzing; and

the unformed, vaguely agitated noise seems to be waiting, too, for something to fall into it and divide it up.

The shout of the dictator is what the noise is waiting for. The clear, piercing voice of the dictator and the universal noise correspond to each other. One produces the other, one is impossible without the other.

What the dictator says is quite unimportant: what matters is the loudness and clearness of what he says. Man now has a landmark from which he gathers that he exists. Previously he was merely a part of the vague noise of words, but now he is a part of a clear, mechanized language.

The mechanized language of the dictator is so much merely a shouting without any real content that when a dictator invades a country, it is as though the essential thing were not the expansion of the frontiers of the invading country but the expansion of the shouting. The aim is to shout down, to destroy by shouting the silence out of the foreign country, to destroy its silent reality, to throw the noise of shouting where the silence was before.

The mechanized language of the dictator is a part of the general verbal noise, but the exaggerated coarseness, the brutal aggressiveness, and the war of invasion correspond to it as well. The noise is so unformed that it is always waiting for something clearly formed to fall into. The man who has become lost in the noise is as it were saved by the firm structure of war, even by the firm structure of a brutal action. That is why it is so easy to make war and to commit brutalities in the world of noise. War and bombs are absorbed by the vacuum of this world of noise.

As in the beginning of time, words precede actions almost inaudibly (man tones down words because he sees that words produce actions as if by magic), so, at the end of time, actions occur once again almost without accompanying words, but now because the word has lost the power of creativity: it has been destroyed.

6

Just as the word no longer arises by a special act of creation, but exists all the time as a continual noise, so human actions no longer happen as a result of special decision, but as part of a continuous process. The process is now the primary, man is a mere appendage of the process. This "labour process" is so secure that it does not seem to depend on man at all: it seems to be a kind of natural phenomenon, almost independent of man altogether. And this never-ending process that is somehow outside man's control, corresponds absolutely to the never-ending

process of noise. This labour process penetrates
everything so much that it seems to continue
inaudibly even in the intervals of work.

The point is not the purpose of the labour
process, but the fact that it never stops. Just as
the word is ground down in the general noise,
so the creative energy of man is stamped out in
this labour process. There is no human purpose
left in this never-ending labour process. A new
kind of being has arisen here, a pure being without purpose, which is taken for granted only
because of its apparent continuity. It is taken
so much for granted that it is not discussed at
all. And that is the great power of the labour
process: that it has established itself outside the
sphere of discussion.

Nothing much is gained by adding improve-
ments to it. The whole labour process today is a
falsification, and therefore not to be improved
by alterations. On the contrary, such alterations
give the impression that the whole process is
real and improvable, and they therefore give it a
false legitimacy.

7

Even more than the labour process, the machine is the embodiment of the never-ending,
sterile uniformity of the world of verbal noise.

The machine is noise turned into iron and
steel. And just as the noise never dares to stop—
as if it were afraid that it might disappear if it

were not always to be occupying the whole of space, so there is a like fear in the machine that it might be made to vanish like a ghost if it were not always convincing itself of its own existence by being in constant motion.

Today man no longer believes in an enduring life after death, but as a substitute he lays claim to some kind of vague continuity that seems to be guaranteed by the never-ending process of noise, labour, and technics. In the machine constantly in motion, there is a kind of pseudo-eternity. It is as though man himself would cease to be manifest if the machine stopped moving. In a world in which there is no other kind of eternity, there is at least the continuous, never-ending movement of the machine.

In a factory it is as though silence was being poured into the empty spaces between the iron bars and manufactured into noise. It is as though the great machines were intending to grind down all the silence of earth—in fact, as though they had already ground it down and were now engaged merely in the last motions of digestion. The machines stand there in triumph, as if they were now considering a new campaign of destruction after the completion of the destruction of silence.

The machine at rest fills up the space in which it stands even more than when it is in motion. Everything belongs to it now. The very air and the stillness seem hard with steel.

The stillness that exists when machines stop working is no silence but an emptiness. Therefore there is an emptiness in the worker's life after the day's work in the factory. The emptiness of the machine follows him home. That is the true cause of his suffering, the real oppression. The peasant, on the other hand, continues to live in the silence in which he has worked, after his work is over. The workman is mute, the peasant silent.

People have spoken of "the world of the working class", the "world of the machine". But the machine that thrusts the worker into the emptiness in which it is itself, is no world, but the end of a world, and the end of a world is quite unable to fill a man with happiness, but only with sadness and despair. That is why the worker can never be content with the machine as a source of happiness.

Man can never be helped by the machine, because it removes him from that realm of time which is a moment of eternity. The continuously moving machine makes a mechanized duration of time, in which there is no autonomous moment, no "atoms of eternity". This mechanized duration has no relationship of any kind to time: it does not fill time but space. Time seems to be stuck fast and transformed into space.

Thus man is separated from time. That is why he is so lonely when faced with the machine, which makes him merely a creature of space.

And instead of time moving, only space seems to be moving with the motions of the machine. Thus man lives only in space, as in a shaft without end digging its way ever deeper through the machine.

In this world of the machine, the word of the poet can never be born, for the word of the poet comes from silence, not from noise. All the machine-poetry of today seems to have been punched out of metal by the machine itself.

And the god who is possible in this machine world is a god manufactured by the machine itself: in the truest sense of the word the *deus ex machina*.

8

In this world of noise the important thing for man is not reality but possibility. Possibilities are not something firmly established and clearly seen, but move from one vagueness to another. They have no beginning and no end. They are not unambiguous but rather like a vague buzzing. Just as the word and true reality belong to each other, so noise and possibility belong together.

The world of noise is also the world of experiment. An experiment is by its very nature not completed, not clearly defined. It does not arise by reason of a definite act, independent of other

acts. It is not like an autonomous phenomenon
but only like the continuation of other experiments, a variation of them, just as one verbal
noise is merely the continuation of other noises.
Therefore experiments never stop: they go on
automatically. And man becomes merely the
laboratory assistant, who is permitted to write
down whatever they choose to communicate
to him.

The way in which things are bound together
today by the law of cause and effect in such a
manner that things are only material for this
law—this process is also a pendant to the verbal
noise.

This is not intended as an attack on the law
of cause and effect itself. The law of cause and
effect is necessary; it is a part of the human
structure. And there is also a readiness in things
themselves to be bound to each other according
to the laws of causality. But this relationship
must not become autonomous, it must not exist
for its own sake, but must be for the sake of
things and for the sake of man.

It is the method of psychoanalysis, of depth
psychology, and a great part of the rest of
psychology, to analyse a phenomenon into an
infinite series of explanations. The phenomenon
becomes covered with explanations and disappears in them. Just as the word falls to pieces

in the general noise of words, so a phenomenon
or a fact falls to pieces in the process of explanation. Just as there are no longer any clearly
defined words, but only the vague noise of words,
so there are no longer any clear phenomena or
clear facts, but only vague explanations of phenomena and facts.

There is a kind of mechanism of explanation
at work today which operates automatically and
draws all phenomena into its activity. Phenomena
have become nothing but material for this machinery of explanation. It is as though everything had been explained in advance—even before the actual appearance of the phenomenon
itself. It is not the explanation that is sought
in order to explain the phenomenon, but the
phenomenon that is sought as material for the
ready-made explanation.

Phenomena are dissolved into nothing by
psychoanalytical and depth-psychological explanations. For example, the phenomena of father,
mother, and son are destroyed by the explanations of psychoanalysis: Oepidus murdered his
father and became the husband of his mother.
These monstrous facts and the phenomena of
father, mother, and son are reduced by psychoanalysis to the mere appendage of an erotic
complex. Whereas Sophocles makes the phenomenon of fatherhood plain for the first time
through the murder, it becomes clear as a basic,
elemental phenomenon: a *father* has been slain

—a father! And the incest of the son with his mother destroys the image of the mother in the actual moment of the incest, it is true. But it rises clearer than ever before through the son's expiation. It becomes the image of the basic phenomenon of motherhood. Not Oedipus but fate itself seems to be wringing out its eyes so that it does not have to see how in the extremes of suffering (not in the extremes of explanation) father, mother, and son die and rise again.

The elemental phenomena of fatherhood and motherhood exist even more firmly and securely after this tragedy. The earth seems to be created more securely than before. The elemental phenomena seem to have been given to the earth for the first time.—But psychoanalysis takes them from the earth and dissolves them with the whole world.

Contemporary existential philosophy is an attempt to get right away from the mechanism of verbal noise and things.

Man throws himself into nothingness. He prefers to be thrown into nothingness than to be a mere part of the mechanism of words and things. Through this fall the mechanism seems to be interrupted, and man having arrived at nothingness stands faced with a new beginning.

But the man who might be faced with a new beginning does not exist at all. He does not exist at all in this nothingness: he is dissolved in it.

There is no human person left to approach the elemental things through the categories of existential philosophy, things such as dread, care, death. There is only an empty space in which man and dread and care and death are all immersed in a single, all-dissolving nothingness. Man is in an empty waste. He himself is this empty waste, in which the echoes of the world of noise are heard even more loudly than before.

Existential philosophy has something of the quality of a subterranean drill, and the noise of this machine is part of the general world of noise.

9

In this universal noise, in which the content of words is no longer valid or important, but only their purely acoustic movements, and in which everything is covered and levelled down by noise, both the word of the poet and the idle chatter of gossips are immersed, swallowed up in the one all-pervading noise.

Here there is neither solitude nor true community; only a jumble in the noise.

Two objects fundamentally opposed to each other no longer stand face to face, they simply slide by each other in the noise.

There are no longer any polarities and therefore no longer any passion, any destiny. What appears as destiny or fate is simply the condensation of many noises into a single enormous din (the din of Nazidom for example). But that is really nothing more than a temporary breakdown, an interruption in the flow of noise.

Imagination is no longer necessary here: the noise has everything in stock.

Truth does not need to be transformed into lies when anyone wants to lie, for truth and falsehood are no longer distinct from each other in the noise.

Life here is an emerging from the noise, and death a disappearing therein.

Through the machinery of verbal noise, however, more evil than good is spread abroad, for the phenomena of evil correspond to the structure of noise and its uncertainty and vagueness than do the phenomena of goodness. Goodness is almost always clearly defined and demarcated. Evil on the other hand loves the vagueness of twilight. In the twilight it can steal in everywhere.

Verbal noise is not evil itself, but it prepares the way for evil: the spirit easily becomes submerged in the noise.

The evil that arises in the noise is different, however, from the evil of, for example, Richard III. It is in man before he has made a decision for evil, before he has even noticed its presence inside him.

The relationship of this evil to the noise is like that of the marsh plant to the marsh: they belong to each other from the very outset; where one is there is the other also. Marsh plant and marsh, falsehood and noise—one is the expression of the other.

It is quite true, of course, that the simple things still survive in the world of noise: birth and death and love. But they exist in a world bereft of words, as pure phenomena, and solitary in the midst of all the machinery. And there is a radiance about them—nowhere so brilliant as here— as if they were trying to burn the machinery all around them in the fire of their radiance.

A radiance goes out from the phenomena of love and death and children. The radiance passes from one phenomenon to another, and in this radiance they cease to be alone. In it they are connected one with another: through the radiance these things speak with one another. Where the word has been destroyed, this radiance has become the language of the elemental things.

THE RADIO

I

THE NOISE of words today is not merely a small part of the world, for a whole world, the world of radio, is based upon it.

Radio is a machine producing absolute verbal noise. The content hardly matters any longer; the production of noise is the main concern. It is as though words were being ground down by radio, transformed into an amorphous mass.

There is no silence in radio or true words either, for a situation has been created in which silence is no longer missed and words are no longer missed either, in which words are ground down to a mere radio-noise, in which everything is present and at the same time nothing is present.

Radio has occupied the whole space of silence. There is no silence any longer. Even when the radio is turned off the radio-noise still seems to go on inaudibly. Radio-noise is so amorphous that it seems to have no beginning and no end; it is limitless. And the type of man formed by the constant influence of this noise is the same: formless, undecided inwardly and externally, with no definite limits and standards.

There is no longer any space in which it is possible to be silent, for space has all been occupied now in advance. It is as if men were afraid that silence might break out somewhere and destroy the noise of radio. And so all space is filled with noise, it dares not be silent, it is constantly on guard against silence.

There is no more silence, only intervals between radio-noises.

Not only what exists already but also what will exist in the future is occupied by radio in advance. Man is accompanied by the noise of the present into a future which is also noise and which is therefore already familiar to him before it actually takes place. Both the present and the future bore him because he already knows what is coming.

In this world of radio-noise there is no present. What the radio transmits is never directly present to man; the object is never directly present. Everything on the radio is constantly on the move, in a state of perpetual flux; nothing is concretely fixed and stable. Past, present and future are all mixed up together in one long drawn-out noise.

Therefore the noise of radio destroys man. Man who should confront objects concretely is deprived of the power of present concrete experience.

This is what makes the man who lives in this world of radio so bad-tempered, so ill at ease: everything is thrown at him by the radio but nothing is really there at all. Everything slips away from him.

Past, present and future are all mixed up together in this world. Everything that might happen in the future is already contained in the mixture, and that is what makes the man who lives in this world of radio so hopeless.

This never-ending noise of radio that is always the same and taken for granted everywhere, comes to impress man by its very continuity and matter-of-courseness as something natural, like the never-ending murmuring of water and the wind—just as natural and inevitable as that. The opposite of the natural—this radio-noise—is able to appear as natural as the sounds of nature herself! And this "natural" noise that has arisen because of man's spiritual defection constantly appeals to the merely physical, to the merely instinctive and vitalistic in man.

Radio is not like something made by man, *it* makes man. It is not something that proceeds from man, it is something that comes to man, surrounds him and covers him. Man has become merely an appendage of the noise of radio. Radio produces the noise and man imitates the motion of the noise. It is his only life.

Radio fills everything and produces everything—all human feeling and wishing and knowing, and even man himself as a person. Man is produced by the radio, experiences himself through the radio for the first time. Just as some people need another person or an occupation to make sure that they still exist themselves, so many people first become aware of themselves today through the radio. But whereas it needs a personal action in order to establish a relationship to another person or to an occupation, radio is available all the time, even before a man has decided that that is what he wants to make sure he is alive. And *it* establishes the relationship, not the person.

It seems as if man can establish a connection between himself and the world only through the mediacy of radio.

Everything comes to him through the radio. Anything or any opinion you want to force on man you need only get included in the general mixture of radio-noise and it will be accepted, for everything can be insinuated into man through the radio.

2

Radio-noise is therefore the new reality, and only what is contained in the noise, only what takes place through the mediacy of radio, is of any worth. An event seems real only when it is part of the noise produced by radio, when it comes out of it. A bomb explodes before you, a factory collapses, and the event enters the retina of the eye but it is hardly noticed in actual fact until it is taken up into the universal noise of radio. Anything you see yourself by yourself with your own eyes is suspect and does not become a real event until you hear it as part of the noise coming from the radio set.

This noise therefore falsifies the direct relationship between the person and the object. Radio entirely destroys the proper mode of knowledge and experience.

What is this "proper mode of knowledge"? When we are listening to someone or when we are reading, the act of listening and reading seems to be an unrepeatable, unique and living action. In such listening and reading, truth presents itself as something unique and therefore personal. But the knowledge thrown at us by the radio is *mechanically* repeatable; the personal element is lacking both in the act of communication and in the act of listening. Radio destroys the basic character of knowledge, which should come from man and be for man. Statements can be transmitted by radio, but a statement is not a truth, for it is essential to truth not only that an object is revealed but that the truth revealed in the object shall be related to man.

The truth that is brought to us by reading or by *direct* personal encounter has an immediate personal reference: the reader or the listener is called upon to reconstruct, as he reads or listens, the intellectual process that the speaker or the writer has already completed. By listening or reading the direct relationship to the object is preserved intact. It is this natural relationship that is lacking in the radio. The knowledge that the radio transmits seems to have been completed once and for all; the listener is not summoned to repeat the process; the facts are simply squeezed into the person listening like so much material into empty boxes. It is as though they neither came from nor were intended for human beings at all. The meaning of knowledge is falsified by the radio.

3

We have said that only what appears as part of the noise of the radio is considered as having any value. But not only are events seen in the guise in which they come through the radio, but they are experienced like that from the start, as if they were already the property of the radio, even *before* they come through the radio. The inhuman thing about all this is that events are often prepared for radio presentation from the very start. Sometimes, for example, events in war are not allowed to run as they would, left to themselves, but are modified with a view to their presentation through the radio. What takes place is not what really is happening, but what it is intended shall happen, what can become noise on the radio. This is what we may call the suspension of all reality.

This is the reason modern war is so monstrous: its terrible reality is not seen in itself, but only as part of the noise of radio. It does not stand concretely before the human mind in itself and therefore it is not properly controlled. Perhaps war is becoming more and more violent and terrible today because it wants to be seen as what it really is, to be seen quite clearly as the terrible thing it really is and not as a mere part of the noise of the radio.

In times in which the power of silence was still effective, war was heard from the background of silence, and against this background it became absolutely clear. There was still an elemental simplicity in its terrors, and its noise subsided again in the death that it brought in its train. In these earlier forms of war man simply suffered it in silence. It was not an object for discussion, but an elemental experience.

Today war is not even a rebellion against silence; it is merely the biggest whirl of noise in the general noisy bustle of life. If war reports were not blaring out from the radio every minute of the day the cannon fire and the wails of the dying would be heard everywhere. In the silence the wails of the dying would be heard and they would weigh down even the sound of the guns. In the silence the war would be heard so loud that it would become intolerable. But the constant noise of the war reports levels down the sound of the guns and the cries of the dying to the general and universal noise. War becomes a part of the general noise of radio, adapted to it; and as a result it is taken for granted like everything that appears in the noise of radio.

It is as though the many and great deaths that take place today were an attempt to restore a zone of silence. When the noise-machine reaches a maximum as it does today, then silence shows itself as a maximum of death.

4

Radio is autonomous noise itself. It has occupied all space: man has been pushed to the edge of space and he can only worm his way through a few remaining gaps and crevices in space.

At six in the morning he is called to early morning physical jerks, at 6.20 to a piece of music, at 7 to news from all over the world, then again to music. At 8 he is called to prayer. At half past eight he is surrounded by recipes for housewives, at 9 by Bach and so on. The radio machine does not seem to be in the least dependent on man at all. It is as though it were just listening to itself all the time. A pianoforte piece by Chopin is answered by some jazz and this in its turn by a talk about vitamins. Radio

seems to be engaged in a conversation with itself. Man has been pushed on one side; he is
simply a machine-hand attending to the radio
noise-machine.

The whole world has become radio-noise.
Anything that is not usable on the radio is cast
out, rejected. The radio is so powerful that you
can pass outside a house and hear a Tschaikovsky
symphony coming out of the window, then go
on a few steps and out of the window of the
next house the same music can still be heard. This
same music is present everywhere, wherever you
go. It is omnipresent. It is as though you had not
moved on at all, but had been standing on the
same spot, although in fact you were moving
all the time. The reality of movement is made
unreal. The noise of radio seems to be independent of space and time, and as much taken
for granted as the air we breathe.

Radio noise is penetrating everywhere, and
all the time it has the appearance of continuity.
It gives its appearance of continuity to man, and
as a result man, who is in fact lacking in continuity, does not realize that he is lacking in
continuity. His own inward discontinuity disappears behind the constant flow of the radio—
which is nothing but the continuity of discontinuity. The difference between continuity and
discontinuity has been removed, just as all dif-

ferences and distinctions vanish in the noise of
radio.

Through the continuity of radio-noise, therefore, man is inspired with a false sense of security.
He is led to imagine that the radio represents
something continuous and that he is himself
continuous. A man goes to his work: radio ac-
companies him, it surrounds him at his work.
He goes to sleep, and radio-noise is the last thing
in his consciousness before he sleeps. He wakes
up, and radio-noise is there again, as if it were
something quite independent of man altogether,
something more real than man himself, and the
guarantee of his own continuity. It is always
around him, always available, the one thing that
seems always ready to care for him, to provide
for him.

God, the eternally Continuous, has been de-
posed, and continuous radio-noise has been in-
stalled in His place. And the fact that although it
is a discovery of man it nevertheless seems to be
independent of him, gives it an appearance of
twilight mysticism.

It has been said that man need not necessarily
become discontinuous through the influence of
radio, that he is free after all to select the pro-
grammes that suit him. I remember a speaker in
a debate on the death penalty in the 1930's in
Baden-Baden stating that he could not understand why there was so much talk about the

death penalty, since it is not the moment in which death comes which is painful but rather the fear of death, and the delinquent was still free to be afraid or not to be afraid as he wished. In just the same way we are free to select from the radio programme what would assure the continuity of our inner life.

In this pseudo-continuity man forgets that everything of essential value is brought into being by a particular, limited, creative act, and he completely loses touch with the spontaneous element in life. This is the wicked thing about radio. None of the elemental phenomena of life, such as truth, loyalty, love, faith, can exist in this world of radio-noise, for these elemental phenomena are direct, clearly defined and clearly limited, original, firsthand phenomena, while the world of radio is the world of the circuitous, the involved, the indirect. In such a world the elemental phenomena are ruined.

5

Many people think that radio can educate man to appreciate the true, the good, and the beautiful, but it must be remembered that it is not the true word that man meets here but the noise of words in which the good, the true, and the beautiful only come to the surface to disappear again. The content of the programme is merely something with which to fill in the noise. The good, the true, and the beautiful are levelled down in the general noise in which all real differences and distinctions are blurred.

It is said that the peasant on a lonely, isolated farm is enabled to take part in the wider life of the nation through the radio. But this more general life into which the peasant is taken up is not the organic life of the community to which the individual can join his own concrete life and enlarge it by so doing, but rather an abstraction from real life in which the individual is diminished and dissolved.

The solitude of the mountains is a concrete reality within the peasant in a lonely mountain village. He is identified with and he is the incarnation of the solitude of nature. This concreteness, this image of the mountains in the peasant, is destroyed by the radio, which makes the peasant a levelled-down part of an abstraction that has the appearance of representing something universal because it is vague. But it is only vaguely, not really, universal.

Man is no longer aware of the radio-noise all around him. He does not hear the constant hum of the radio: it has become a kind of noisy silence of which he hardly takes any notice at all, however loud it may be all around him.

This is a sign of the deepest possible contempt

for language, that this constant stream of words is allowed to be turned on and no attention paid to it.

Radio educates man *not* to listen to words, which means not to listen to man speaking. And therefore it takes man away from the Thou, and from Love.

Man ought to be sad to think that he has lost contact with the true word. But radio-noise fills up the space within him where the word used to be, and man does not notice that the word has been taken away from him. He does not notice it but it is noticed in him without his knowledge, and that makes him restless and nervous.

It seems to me that this is the cause of many modern psychoses: an unlimited mass of words is thrown into us through the radio, words that really demand an answer. But there are too many words for an answer to be possible, and no answer is even expected, for at every moment a new mass of words is thrown out.

The people who still know somehow or other that an answer must be given to everything that is brought before the human mind become confused. They feel that an answer ought to be given, but there is no time and no room in which it can be given, and out of this confusion of mind a psychosis can very easily develop which may show itself in all kinds of inhibitions. Such a psychosis may serve as an escape from a

world that has taken the most essential thing in
life from man: his power to answer and to be
responsible.

6

Wireless sets are like constantly firing auto-
matic pistols shooting at silence.

Behind all this noise the enemy lurks in hiding:
silence.

The noise of radio is becoming more and
more violent, because the fear is becoming more
and more acute that it may be suddenly attacked
by silence and the real word.

Sometimes, when above all the noise of radio
one sees the silence of the heavens above and in
the silence the all-absorbing Light, absorbing
almost the walls of heaven, then one holds one's
breath half in fear and half in joy lest in the
very next moment the noise of the radio may be
absorbed by this light and disappear therein.

THE REMAINS OF SILENCE

I

IT IS AS THOUGH the last residuum of silence were to be destroyed; as though an order had been made for a census of the residue of silence in every person and in every house, and for that residue to be exterminated, as an enemy.

Aeroplanes scour the sky for the silence encamped behind the clouds. The propeller beats are like so many blows against the silence.

The great cities are like enormous reservoirs of noise. Noise is manufactured in the city, just as goods are manufactured. The city is the place where it is always kept in stock, completely detached from the object from which it came. It broods over the city and falls down on men and things.

But in the night, when the lights are out, the streets seem like shafts down which the noise has fallen and in which it has disappeared. Men and things doze wearily, as they are no longer filled with the noise. People roam along by the houses like shadows, and the walls of the houses seem like the front walls of enormous dilapidated and disintegrated tombs.

In sleep, however, with their ears on the

pillow, men seem to be listening to the depths of the earth, to the vanished noise or perhaps to the vanished silence.

The great city is a fortress against the silence, around which destruction hovers in its feverish activity. There is a striving towards destruction, a search for death, a search for the silence after death.

Silence no longer exists as a *world*, but only in fragments, as the remains of a world. And as man is always frightened by remains, so he is frightened by the remains of silence.

Sometimes in a city a man suddenly collapses and dies in the midst of the noise of the highway. It is then as if all at once the shreds of silence, still lying around, amongst the tree tops by the roadside, suddenly descend on the dead man. It is as if these remains of silence had crept down to the silence of the dead man in the roadway, and there is a momentary stillness in the city. The remains of silence are with the fallen man in order to disappear with him into death, to disappear through the fissure of death. The dead man takes the last remains of silence with him.

2

Silence is no longer taken for granted. When it is still sometimes found in a person, it seems like a museum piece or a phantom.

Christine B. was perfect when she sat in silence: everything was then right about her. She was like a peasant woman running a big farm simply by being there herself. When Christine B. sat there saying nothing, one knew the words that were coming out unheard from the silence. One hearkened for those words, one was with Christine B., and at the same time in the distant place where those words coming from the silence seemed to become sound. One was, through the magic of this silence, here and at the same time in a distant place.

But as soon as Christine B. spoke, her words were noisy, and she, too, the whole woman, was noisy. It was as though she did not possess the silence that was in her at all. She moved about so nervously, as though it were not merely not in her but as though there were no silence left anywhere.

Christine certainly still had silence within her, but it was utterly isolated from her, shut off from the word, and therefore shut off from the person. The words were living a life of their own, and the silence was living a life of its own: it was lonely. Words and silence were so isolated from one another in her that it seemed as if when she spoke, only words were present in her, and when she was silent only silence. In the silence Christine was cut off from her own words, and so utterly permeated by the silence that it seemed as if she were demonically possessed by the last remains of silence in the world. She sat there like a ghost of silence within the noise of the others.

3

It is true that in the world of noise there are still words that come from the world of silence, but they are lonely in the world of noise, and the silence that is round the edge of such words is shot through with melancholy. The words seem to come from the dark ground of melancholy, not from the darkness of silence. Like the black-edged butterfly, the Camberwell Beauty, such lonely words hover around in the world of noise.

It is true that in the world of noise there are still words that come from the world of silence, but like ancient treasures excavated from the earth they belong to a different world. The men of noise are frightened for a moment when they hear such authentic words, and this moment of fright is also a moment of silence—until the massive steam roller of noise arrives to level down the word and the silence, to take them with it and destroy them.

Such words, which retain an authentic relationship to silence in the midst of the noise—it is as if the god himself were to step forth from the white marble of an excavated statue. For a moment men, cars, and planes would stand still; the sudden appearance of the god would be like a halt-sign to everything on the move. But in the very next moment a car would come along and carry the god away and disappear with him in the noisy traffic that would have already started up again, and the god would become a mere tiny part of the noisy, moving traffic.

It is true that silence, as a world of its own, has been destroyed; sound has occupied everything; the earth seems to belong to it. There is no world unity of the spirit or of religion or politics. But there is a world unity of noise. In it all men and all things are connected one with another.

But these still remain: the quietness of dawn, and the furtive fall of night.

Never was the silence of these things more perfect than now; never was it more beautiful. The silence of these things is lonely: the power of silence, which once went out from them to the other things of earth and to men, is now confined to itself. Things are silent for themselves. One poor man once said to another: "Nobody gives me his respects, so I give myself my own respects, on my own". So are these things: no one gives them silence, no one takes it from them. They give it to themselves and have it for themselves alone.

ILLNESS, DEATH AND SILENCE

1

MAN TODAY is without sleep because he is without silence. In sleep a man returns with the silence that is in him back into the great silence of the universe. But man lacks the silence today which used to lead him back into the great silence of the universe. Sleep today is only a tiredness caused by noise, a reaction to the noise. It has ceased to be a world of its own.

"Even the sleeping work as they co-operate with what is happening in the universe." (Heraclitus)

2

Even in the world of noise there is a silence surrounding illness, a silence that all the talking, right and wrong, of the doctors cannot dispel. It is as though silence, driven away from everywhere else, had come to hide with the sick. It lives with them as if in the catacombs.

Often when a patient is lying silently, it is as though the sick person were merely the place where silence has settled. The illness came, followed by the silence. It seems like a pathway on which room was made for silence. It slowly occupies the whole body, and the words of the sick one and those of the visitor can hardly penetrate the silence.

Silence has always been present with the sick. And yet the silence that is present with the sick today is not the same as in former ages. The silence that is present with the sick today is uncanny, for it should be a part of healthy normal life and has now been driven out of healthy life and lives only with the sick.

Noise has now entered into that good part of life which used to belong to silence, but silence has taken refuge in that evil part of life—the world of sickness and disease, and silence now approaches man on these evil subterranean ways. The silence that used to be the salvation and the healing of man has become a menace and a calamity.

There are diseases that are like vengeful silence itself: the silence that is vengeful because it has been expelled and can only break through to man out of the dark caverns of disease. Cancer is such a disease. It is surrounded by silence. This does not mean that the origin of the disease is still wrapped in silence, but that man is much more diseased by cancer than all the symptoms show, which are only like symptoms of an evil silence.

3

Professor L. was forced by a stroke to speak very slowly. He did not regard it as a loss that his words found difficulty in emerging from the silence into sound. He said that previously it had been an easy matter for him to speak; words had come all too easily, jumping quickly from one to the other, and never rising slowly from the silence. But now because of this illness it was quite an event for a word to become a sound. It was like a new creation every time he was able to bring a word out of the silence. It was the same with him as with medieval man, for whom every movement from silence into speech was an event in itself. What he had never achieved in a state of health—the experience of the birth of words from silence as the extraordinary event that it is—he had now been able to make a personal experience because of his illness.

In this way Professor L. overcame his illness. And not only that, but he became more through his illness than he had been before it.

4

The flowers, the fields, and the mountains stood in all their vivid reality before us, as if they would remain forever thus and as if there would be no need of anyone to remember them when they passed quietly into winter.

A man stood looking at them and thought of his own death and of how he would one day see all this no more.

In the moment in which he thought of death, he was jolted out of this present reality, and looked at the flowers, the meadow, and the trees as if already from the land of death. They now looked as if he were seeing them through the wrong end of a telescope: far away and very tiny, like toys, and hovering in the distance. They were beautiful as never before, and he waited anxiously for them to become smaller and smaller until they should fade away into the land of death where he was now.

The movement of the spirit which enabled this man to see the present from the past, from the land of death, is only possible when there is much silence in a man. Then the silence leads the soul from the present into the distant land of death, and the spirit does not feel itself forsaken, but moves along the wall of silence, moves along and clings to the wall of silence.

5

Whatever we have in our home and heart, whatever we are before God and man, whatever we need in field and wood, in kitchen and cellar, it is the experiences and inventions, the acquisitions and discoveries of the dead which stand us in good stead, on which we rely and depend in order to achieve higher and better things. Thus each one of us has a part in the vast inheritance from the past, and unless a man is sick with frantic arrogance, he will thank those who have gone before him for all the pains, the fruits of which we are now harvesting in such abundance. (Gotthelf)

Man is only in relation with this world of the dead, if he is already in relation with the world of silence. It is only in the silence in his own life that he hears again the words of the dead. Then the dead carry the silence into the world of man, the world of the word. They give it some of the power that is in silence. And they make men and things receptive to the power that comes from silence.

Today death is no longer a world of its own, it is merely the last residue of life—used up life, and not even silence belongs to it any longer. Silence is only as it were loaned to it, loaned out of pity.

Yet all at once death may appear again as a whole world of its own, and life seem a mere prelude to this world. It can appear in the guise of war, and as the millions of deaths in war are not able to bring silence, the horrors of war bring it instead. The silence that has been expelled from life and from death then comes through the stupor of terror.

Precisely because death makes us feel the mysteries of the world most acutely, it should be the last thing in the world we should use to make life more difficult for each other. Let us rather respect death as the clearest symbol of our community in the silence, the symbol that hangs as an inescapable fate over us all. (Overbeck)

THE WORLD WITHOUT SILENCE

NOTHING HAS changed the nature of man so much as the loss of silence. The invention of printing, technics, compulsory education—nothing has so altered man as this lack of relationship to silence, this fact that silence is no longer taken for granted, as something as natural as the sky above or the air we breathe.

Man who has lost silence has not merely lost one human quality, but his whole structure has been changed thereby.

Formerly silence covered all things: man had first to break through the covering of silence before he could get close to an object, and the silence protected even the thoughts he wanted to think himself. Man could not throw himself directly at things and ideas: they were shielded by the silence surrounding them, and man was protected from moving towards them all too quickly. The silence was stationed in front of things and ideas. It was there objectively. It was encamped there like a defending army. Man moved slowly and quietly towards ideas and things. The silence was always present between the movement from one idea to another, from one thing to another. The rhythm of the silence punctuated the movement.

Every movement became a special act: the silence, the primitive rock of silence had to be removed before one could move forward. But then when one had arrived at an idea, one was really there with the idea, and the idea or the thing really existed for the first time. The concrete reality was, as it were, created in the direct personal encounter with man.

Today man no longer moves deliberately to ideas and things. They are absorbed into his own emptiness, they rush at him, they swirl around him. Man no longer thinks, he has his thinking done for him. *Cogito, ergo sum* has been replaced by *cogitor, ergo non sum*.

The earth was once no less occupied than it is today, but it was occupied by silence, and man was unable to seize everything in it as it was all held fast by silence. Man did not need to know everything: the silence knew it all for him. And as man was connected with the silence, he knew many things through the silence.

The heaven of silence no longer covers the world of ideas and things today, restraining them with its weight and pressure. Where it used to be there is now an empty space, and things are as it were drawn up by suction into the space where the silence used to dwell. Things are exposed, uncovered and pressing upwards. More and more things are constantly pushing their way upwards, and that is the real "revolt of the masses", this rebellion of things and ideas that are no longer held down by the pressure of silence.

Man is not even aware of the loss of silence: so much is the space formerly occupied by the silence so full of things that nothing seems to be missing. But where formerly the silence lay on a thing, now one thing lies on another. Where formerly an idea was covered by the silence, now a thousand associations speed along to it and bury it.

In this world of today in which everything is reckoned in terms of immediate profit, there is no place for silence. Silence was expelled because it was unproductive, because it merely existed and seemed to have no purpose.

Almost the only kind of silence that there is today is due to the loss of the faculty of speech. It is purely negative: the absence of speech. It is merely like a technical hitch in the continuous flow of noise.

There is still perhaps a little silence; a little is still tolerated. Just as the almost completely exterminated Indians are still allowed a little living space in their miserable reservations, so silence is sometimes allowed a chink of space in the sanatoria between two and three in the afternoon: "An hour of silence" and in the "two minutes' silence" in which the masses must be silent "in

remembrance of . . ." But there is never a special silence in memory of the silence that is no
more.

It is true that silence still exists as a true silence
in monastic communities. In the Middle Ages the
silence of the monks was still connected with the
silence of other men outside the monastery. Today the silence in the monasteries is isolated; it
lives literally only in monastic seclusion.

THE HOPE

THE HOUSES of the great city are like pillboxes against the silence. It is as though shots were being fired from their windows against the silence.

At night the houses and squares seem to be raised aloft by the lights, no longer firmly on the ground, but hovering in the air. It is as though the lights were lifting up the city; like an enormous balloon it seems to hover over itself. More and more lights blaze up, green and blue, and the city seems to hover. But the sky over the city with the stars trembles and flees.

Then all at once the lights go out. A moment of silence arises, and then it is as though the city were considering whether to hurl itself down and destroy itself.

But suddenly from the top floor of a house through a chink come the rays of a friendly light. And then it is as if the rays were being sent out like the dove from Noah's ark to see whether it is not time for the city to land on the mount of silence. But the rays of light return to the top floor of the house. Their mission was in vain—until the moon comes and before it disappears toward morning, takes them into its own rays.

Perhaps silence has not yet been completely destroyed. Perhaps it is still to be found in man, but sleeping. For sometimes it happens that a quality of an individual or a nation is as dead for a long time, covered over by another quality. For example, the poetic creativity of a nation can seem to have died out, overgrown by scientific or political talents. But one day it appears again and so powerfully that it seems to overflow with its fullness back into the space of the empty years. Or perhaps an age is rationalistic, so much so that it seems there will never be anything but rationalism in the future. But suddenly the rationalism disappears and an antirationalist age appears. The metaphysical power in man had not been destroyed; it was not dead but only asleep. It seems that from time to time *one* direction of the spirit has to show itself more clearly and more forcefully than it really wants to, so that the *other* can be hidden and recuperate in peace.

Perhaps it is thus with silence, too. Perhaps it is not dead but merely sleeping, resting. Then noise would be only the wall behind which silence is sleeping, and noise would then be not the victor over silence, not its master, but its servant watching whilst its master, silence, sleeps.

Ah, said Selina, is it not a comforting thought, this hidden wealth in our souls; can we not hope that unconsciously we love God more inwardly than we know, and that a quiet instinct for the second world is working inside us, all the time we give ourselves up so much to the external world. (Jean Paul)

It seems sometimes as though it might come to a fight between silence and noise; as if silence were secretly preparing for an invasion.

Noise is powerful, but sometimes silence seems even more powerful—so powerful that it does not seem to notice whether noise is there or not.

It is true that the noise is always increasing, always gathering more and more things into itself. But perhaps everything is being concentrated in the noise so that it can all be destroyed more easily when silence launches a surprise attack.

Perhaps this enormous mechanism of noise will explode by its own violence, and the report will be a call to the silence telling it that its time has come.

Watchman, what of the night?
Watchman, what of the night?
The watchman said: The morning cometh, also the
     night.
If you seek, seek: return, come.

                                        (Isa. 21:11)

SILENCE AND FAITH

I

THERE IS a relationship between silence and faith. The sphere of faith and the sphere of silence belong together. Silence is the natural basis on which the super-nature of faith is accomplished.

God became man for the sake of man. This event is so utterly extraordinary and so much against the experience of reason and against everything the eye has seen, that man is not able to make response to it in words. A layer of silence lies between this event and man, and in this silence man approaches the silence that surrounds God Himself. Man and the mystery first meet in the silence, but the word that comes out of this silence is original, as the first word before it had ever spoken anything. That is why it is able to speak of the mystery.

It is a sign of the love of God that a mystery is always separated from man by a layer of silence. And that is a reminder that man should also keep a silence in which to approach the mystery. Today, when there is only noise in and around man, it is difficult to approach the mystery. When the layer of silence is missing, the extraordinary easily becomes connected with the ordinary, with the routine flow of things, and man reduces the extraordinary to a mere part of the ordinary, a mere part of the mechanical routine.

What many preachers say about the Mystery of God is often lifeless and therefore ineffectual. What they say comes only from words jumbled up with many thousands of other words. It does not come from silence. But it is in silence that that first meeting between man and the Mystery of God is accomplished, and from silence the word also receives the power to become extraordinary as the Mystery of God is extraordinary. It then rises above the order of ordinary words, just as the Mystery of God rises above the ordinary routine of things. It is as if words had been created for nothing else but the representation of the extraordinary. Thereby they become identical with the extraordinary, with the mystery; and thereby they have a power akin to that of the mystery.

It is true that man is able through the power of the spirit to give an elemental force to words, but the word that comes from silence is already elemental. The human mind has no need to spend itself in giving the word an elemental force that has already been given to it by the silence. The silence helps the spirit in man.

It is possible, too, that man could keep himself in the faith through the spirit, but the spirit would always have to be on the watch, always on guard, and faith would cease to be natural and effortless. And the effort required, not the faith itself, would then appear to be the important thing. A man who made such a great effort to believe might appear to himself as one to whom God Himself has directly committed the faith, as one saddled with the faith by God Himself. And he might seem to himself to be a prophet. It is true that the faith is extraordinary, but what is extraordinary is nothing to do with the external conditions of faith, not the effort required to believe. When the natural basis of silence is lacking, then the external conditions rise indeed to the level of the extraordinary.

2

The silence of God is different from the silence of men. It is not opposed to the word: word and silence are one in God. Just as language constitutes the nature of man, so silence is the nature of God; but in that nature everything is clear, everything is word and silence at the same time.

The voice of God is not a voice of nature, or of all the voices of nature put together, but the voice of silence. As certainly as the whole creation would be dumb if the Lord had not given it the power of speech and as certainly as everything that hath breath should therefore praise the Lord, just as certainly only he hears in all voices the voice of the Lord Himself, who hears the voice that is inaudible. (Wilhelm Vischer)

Sometimes it seems as though man and nature only speak because God has not yet spoken, and as though man and nature are silent because they have not yet heard the silence of God.

The silence of God is transformed by love into the Word. The Word of God is a self-giving silence, giving itself to man.

If a man like Paul "has heard unspeakable words which it is not permitted to man to utter," then this unspeakable word falls like a heavy weight into the silence of man. It makes the silence deeper, and the word that comes from the depths in which that which is unspeakable lies, has a trace of the divinely Unspeakable in it.

I was in the heaven which receives the greatest light and saw things none can say who come down from hence; for our spirit hastens on the paths of its yearning into boundless depths and cannot find its way back. (Dante, Paradiso)

3

In prayer the word comes again of itself into silence. It is from the very outset in the sphere of silence. It is taken up by God, taken away from man; it is absorbed into silence and disappears therein. Prayer can be never-ending, but the word of prayer always disappears into silence. Prayer is a pouring of the word into silence.

In prayer the word rises from silence, just as every real word rises from silence, but it comes out of it only to travel straight to God, to the "voice of the ebbing silence".

In prayer the region of the lower, human silence comes into relation with the higher silence of God; the lower rests in the higher. In prayer the word and therefore man is in the center between two regions of silence. In prayer man is held between these two regions.

Elsewhere, outside prayer, the silence of man is fulfilled and receives its meaning in speech. But in prayer it receives its meaning and fulfillment in the meeting with the silence of God.

Elsewhere, outside prayer, the silence in man serves the word in man. But now, in prayer, the word serves the silence in man: the word leads the human silence to the silence of God.

The present state of the world and the whole of life is diseased. If I were a doctor and were asked for my advice, I should reply: Create silence! Bring men to silence. The Word of God cannot be heard in the noisy world of today. And even if it were blazoned forth with all the panoply of noise so that it could be heard in the midst of all the other noise, then it would no longer be the Word of God. Therefore create silence.

(Kierkegaard)